LONDON BUSES IN THE 1970s

1975-1979: FROM CRISIS TO RECOVERY

LONDON BUSES IN THE 1970s

1975-1979: FROM CRISIS TO RECOVERY

JIM BLAKE

PEN & SWORD
TRANSPORT

AN IMPRINT OF PEN & SWORD BOOKS LTD.
YORKSHIRE – PHILADELPHIA

First published in Great Britain in 2019 by
Pen and Sword Transport
An imprint of
Pen & Sword Books Ltd
Yorkshire - Philadelphia

Copyright © Jim Blake, 2019

ISBN 978 1 47388 716 9

The right of Jim Blake to be identified as Author of this work has been asserted by him in
accordance with the Copyright, Designs and Patents Act 1988.

A CIP catalogue record for this book is available from the British Library.

Typeset by Aura Technology and Software Services, India

Printed and bound in India by Replika Press Pvt. Ltd.

Pen & Sword Books Ltd incorporates the Imprints of Pen & Sword Books Archaeology, Atlas,
Aviation, Battleground, Discovery, Family History, History, Maritime, Military, Naval, Politics,
Railways, Select, Transport, True Crime, Fiction, Frontline Books, Leo Cooper, Praetorian Press,
Seaforth Publishing, Wharncliffe and White Owl.

For a complete list of Pen & Sword titles please contact

PEN & SWORD BOOKS LIMITED
47 Church Street, Barnsley, South Yorkshire, S70 2AS, England
E-mail: enquiries@pen-and-sword.co.uk
Website: www.pen-and-sword.co.uk

or

PEN AND SWORD BOOKS
1950 Lawrence Rd, Havertown, PA 19083, USA
E-mail: Uspen-and-sword@casematepublishers.com
Website: www.penandswordbooks.com

FRONT COVER In many ways, London Country's ageing RF fleet was their saviour during the shortage of serviceable buses, as they could work virtually any route. On 8 June 1976, modernised Green Line RF129, now demoted to bus status, has returned to its original role, working route 704 from Dunton Green Garage at Farnborough Common.

CONTENTS

INTRODUCTION

The second half of the 1970s opened amid a lot of problems for London's buses. Both London Transport and London Country had ageing fleets of RTs and RFs, along with the notoriously unreliable MB and SM class AEC Swift single-deckers. London Transport was also cursed with the dreadful DMS class of Daimler Fleetline double-deckers, then about halfway through its production run. Even the usually reliable Routemasters in both fleets were showing signs of wear and tear.

To add to both operators' woes, a nationwide shortage of vehicle spares from the early years of the decade onwards led to extreme vehicle shortages, exacerbated of course by the frightful unreliability of the MB, SM and DM types – so much so that buses from other operators were borrowed to keep services going from the summer of 1975 onwards. At the same time, London Transport even bought a small batch of redundant British Airways Routemaster coaches, pressing them in to service to replace RTs. As early as 1974, London Transport had thrown in the towel with its MBs, and new DMSs, meant to see the RTs off and then start to replace Routemasters, were used to replace them instead. But they too were just as bad, if not worse! The net result was that surviving RTs had to carry on regardless, and Routemasters continued to have 'as good as new' overhauls at Aldenham throughout the decade.

While a frantic search was made to find a better one-man-operated double-decker than the DMS by London Transport, London Country had begun to take delivery of large numbers of Leyland Nationals, as well as further AN-class Leyland Atlanteans, with the result that they began to withdraw the Routemasters they had inherited from London Transport. The inevitable happened from late 1977 onwards – most of these were bought back by LT, along with the remaining British Airways examples.

By 1979, all of London Transport's MB-types had been withdrawn, excepting a small number retained for 'Red Arrow' services, and the SMs were following rapidly. The same was true of both types in the London Country fleet. Also by now, the first of the dreadful DMSs had reached the scrapyard – before the last RTs were withdrawn in April 1979; that says it all, really. At least better one-man-operated types had finally been found to replace them, in the shape of the M class Metrobuses and the T class Leyland B15 Titans. Deliveries of these got into their stride in the last year of the decade, at last beginning the recovery in London Transport's fortunes that was so desperately needed.

Where London Country was concerned, vehicle type allocations to routes was far less rigid than with London Transport, so that by the middle of the decade, virtually any type could appear on any route, except of course where low bridges or other restricted clearances dictated otherwise. By the end of the decade, only a handful of Routemasters (all of which would pass to London Transport early in 1980) and

MB-types, plus one or two XFs, remained in the fleet of its London Transport heritage, and London Country was fast becoming just another National Bus Company fleet dominated by Leyland Atlanteans and Nationals.

The year 1979 was also, of course, significant politically for both operators. Margaret Thatcher had been elected in May, leading firstly to the destruction of London Transport following its seizure from Greater London Council control, and secondly to the split-up of London Country. Eventually, the remnants of both fleets were privatised – but that's another story.

All of the photographs in this volume are my own. Many show rare and unusual scenes and have not been published before. Historical notes are derived initially from my own records, but I must also thank the London Omnibus Traction Society and the PSV Circle, whose various publications were of great value in building these up. May I also put on records thanks to the website 'Ian's Bus Stop', from which I have had to glean various details of 'post-Reshaping Plan' type vehicles such as the DMS and SNB, which, since I had little interest in them at the time, I did not keep records of.

Jim Blake
3 February 2016

On 23 January 1975, Holloway RM403 sets off from Archway Station terminus for Camberwell on trolleybus replacement route 17, passing Muswell Hill SMS725 on the stand on a short working of route 210. The 17 would be one of a number of routes in this area converted to crew DM operation a few days later, releasing RMs which replaced RTs, mostly in south-east London. Just six years later, most of these routes would revert to RM operation – though the 17 did not, having been withdrawn in October 1978.

One of the routes mentioned above converted to RM was the 1. New Cross RT2106 passes beneath the bridge carrying the long-closed Southwark Park Station in Rotherhithe New Road on 24 January 1975, three days before RMs took over.

On 25 January 1975, brand new Holloway DM1751 calls at Islington Town Hall on its first day in service on pioneer RML route 104. This is one of the batch bodied by Metro-Cammell.

On the same day, another new DM on the 104, 1741, is overtaken in Goswell Road, Angel, by Muswell Hill RML2357 on route 43, which would also convert to crew DM the following Monday (27th).

An oddity seen on Highgate Hill later that day is SCG385M, a Dormobile Pacemaker 16-seater demonstrator being tried out at Holloway Garage on minibus route C11. As things turned out, somewhat larger vehicles would be used to replace its Ford Transits, as will be seen later.

On 5 February 1975, new Holloway crew-operated DM1759 is seen at King's Cross on the weekday 168A, another route converted to this type, though from RT rather than RM. The DMS on route 259 behind is an OPO example, which must have been confusing to passengers since the two routes ran together all the way from Farringdon Street to Finsbury Park.

Brixton RT1560 in Streatham High Road on the Sunday 57A is overheating – at least a driver could see this on an RT, unlike on rear-engined vehicles such as the early DMS from the same garage following on route 50. Seen on 9 February 1975.

Illustrating the serious vehicle shortage problems London Country were suffering at this time, modernised ex-Green Line East Grinstead RF75 stands in for an RML on the busy 409 on 18 February 1975 when seen at West Croydon Station, also with a DMS on route 50 following.

Further south along Croydon High Street, RMC1486, one of Reigate Garage's route 406 allocation, stands in for an RCL on route 414.

RT755 has run in after the morning rush hour to the antiquated Middle Row, North Kensington Garage on 19 February 1975 on the 187, which meandered all the way through back streets from Hampstead Heath to South Harrow at the time. RMs took over this route at the end of the month.

RTs continued to have three-year recertifications and repaints during 1975. On 20 February 1975, RT2240 has just been done and substitutes for a Merton RM on route 49 when seen crossing Tooting Bec Common. This RT would survive to be the penultimate one in service, at Barking in April 1979. It was then preserved, but later butchered to become one of the ridiculous 'triple-deckers' in a Harry Potter film in 2002.

Dunton Green modernised RF48 stands in for an RP on Green Line route 705 when seen at Lewisham Clock Tower on 21 February 1975. Corporate NBC all-green livery did not suit this type of RF.

A well-laden Walworth RT3774 is seen in Falcon Road, Battersea, on 22 February 1975. Most buses on route 45 on this Saturday were RTs, since it was due to convert from RM to crew DM next day and, as Walworth's RTs (allocated for the 176 and 176A) were not used at weekends, they were allocated to it to facilitate the redeployment elsewhere of the garage's RMs.

Next day, the DMs have arrived: brand new Walworth DM1790 is about to set off from King's Cross on the 45's very circuitous journey to South Kensington, via Holborn, Elephant, Camberwell, Brixton, Stockwell, Clapham, Battersea and Chelsea on 23 February 1975.

In the evening of 27 February 1975, timetables are already posted for new services on route 130B on 1 March, when South Croydon RML2756 and 2724 are seen at the route's Vulcan Way terminus on the New Addington industrial estate. New crew DMs will replace the RMLs that day, redeploying them to routes 8, 8A and 88.

Caught amid an unseasonal snowstorm, Sutton RT1572 stands at the Morden Station terminus of route 164A on 18 March 1975.

New crew-operated DMs continued to enter service thick and fast in the spring of 1975. Here at Finsbury Circus, brand new Brixton DM1059, of the Park Royal batch, sets off for Streatham on its first day of service after replacing RTs on route 133 on 23 March 1975. It is a Park Royal-bodied example - these were delivered concurrently with the Metro-Cammell batch. Many of the RTs replaced were retained to bolster services elsewhere.

In the London Country fleet, red MB-types were still helping out at a variety of garages at this period. In Beechen Grove, Watford, Garston MBS59 is seen on 19 April 1975 on local route 346, which had been allocated new green MBSs early in 1969. Interestingly it has no stickers saying it is on hire to London Country, and served the same stops in this area as similar-looking London Transport MBs on route 258 and SMSs on route 142, which must have confused passengers.

Also confusing to passengers is RF70 on route 301 in Beechen Grove on the same occasion - it is anyone's guess as to where it is going! It is a Green Line RF still based at Tring Garage for route 706, so is presumably bound for Aylesbury and is standing in for either an RT or RMC – both types being officially allocated to the long 301 trunk route at this time.

Busy route 347, which ran from Uxbridge to Hemel Hempstead, had been converted from RT to RML operation in the spring of 1966. However, by now, many of Garston's RMLs were off the road due to the spares shortage, and RTs have been drafted in to cover for them. Tring RT994 is on loan to Garston when seen in Clarendon Road, Watford, also on 19 April 1975.

One of the Central Area's busiest routes at this time was trolleybus-replacement route 253, running from Aldgate to Warren Street via the inner-London suburbs of Whitechapel, Bethnal Green, Hackney, Clapton, Stamford Hill, Finsbury Park, Holloway and Camden Town. Much of it served the large Jewish community in the East End and around Stamford Hill, earning it the nickname amongst bus crews and passengers alike of 'The Yiddisher Flyer', not something that would be acceptable today. At weekends, it was operated by crew DMs from Holloway and Stamford Hill Garage (with RMs during the week) and also Clapton RMs on Mondays to Saturdays. I was a conductor at the latter garage at this time, and often worked the route, which was great fun. It was a life-line to the many elderly people along the route, who absolutely *hated* the DMs, and would always let them go by and wait for our RMs. On 20 April 1975, Stamford Hill DM1732 lumbers along Mare Street, Hackney, and is noticeably half empty for this reason. After a while, weekend DM working was abandoned and the RMs returned.

On 22 April 1975, RF168, still in Green Line livery, stands at Amersham Garage after working route 336 from Watford, accompanying withdrawn RF127. Note the LT bus stop flag still fixed to the wall of this typical 1930s London Transport Country Area garage.

Also on 22 April 1975, Two Waters' (Hemel Hempstead) RF246 departs from Hemel Hempstead Station on local route 307A. This is a modernised Green Line RF officially demoted to Country bus status. In retrospect, it is interesting to wonder how London Country would have coped at this time of extreme vehicle shortages without a reserve of these sturdy old vehicles, many of which had recently been made spare upon replacement by new Leyland National Green Line coaches. RFs were able to cover for anything from a small BN-class single-decker to an RML or even an AN in times of need.

To prove the point, another of these vehicles, Garston RF196 on loan to Two Waters, approaches its home garage on trunk route 301, packed with homegoing rush hour commuters. This is another modernised Green Line coach demoted to bus status.

Hemel Hempstead Garage was actually located on the A41 at Two Waters, and here also on 22 April 1975, Tring RT1015 is parked in the garage yard with two withdrawn MBs, MB98 being nearest the camera. The latter had been withdrawn in January and would languish in store until late 1977 when it went for scrap. The RT, theoretically some twenty years older, remained in service until May 1976.

Yet another RF called to the rescue is RF107, standing in for a Garston RML on a rush hour duty of route 311 at Bushey Arches on 30 April 1975. This one, however, was withdrawn in June.

On 2 May 1975, an overheating RT603 accompanies two SMs and an AN in Stevenage Bus Station, one of three that had to be kept at the local garage for rush hour trips on the 303 to Hitchin, owing to the railway bridge at Little Wymondley being too low to take an AN, but just high enough for an RT. This RT was the last to work at Stevenage, a year later.

Oddities that first came to London for the 1975 summer season were a batch of Midland Red-built D9 double-deckers, cut down to open-top for use on London Transport's Round London Sightseeing Tour. They were dubbed class OM and actually owned by Prince Marshall's Obsolete Fleet, operated on hire to LT. OM1 is seen at Trafalgar Square on 4 May 1975. Of note is the apparent 'bullseye' on the radiator which is, however, a similar symbol used by Midland Red. Their D9s were contemporary to London's RMs, to which they were also similar in concept, being both designed by their operator.

East meets west at Kew Green on Whit Monday, 26 May 1975; Kingston RT4412 is one of two which have worked bank holiday extras to this tourist location by the river, whilst the 'Private' RT on the left, occupying their stand, is Barking RT3020 on a staff outing. The busy 65, then running from Ealing to Chessington, converted to RM in October.

This busy scene at Romford Market on 31 May 1975 shows North Street recently-overhauled RM1567 working the one-bus 175A to Ongar, flanked by two Eastern National Bristol FLF Lodekkas and an SMS. The 175A had recently been upgraded from RT, and could not be one-person-operated owing to a three-point reversal turn at its Ongar, Cripsey Avenue terminus.

A more unusual use for a London Country RF was that of a mobile recruiting bus, as shown by RF594 at Epsom Station on 4 June 1975.

This was Derby Day, and also at Epsom Station, East Grinstead XF1 accompanies an RT and two MB-types on racegoers' route 406F. The XF has recently been repainted in NBC corporate livery – which actually suits it!

On the same day, one of several red MBs still on loan for use in the area is MB125, working from Leatherhead Garage on route 418, which ran well into the former Central Area between Tolworth and Kingston. Note its upper-case via points on the blind.

On the same day, Kingston coal yard has now graduated into a parking place for service buses, including those which have been withdrawn. Kingston's own RF516, which will survive here until the end in March 1979, accompanies Stockwell RML2505, which has been out of action owing to the spare parts shortage since December 1974 and will not re-enter service until September 1975, and DMS332, which had recently been delicensed for the same reason and would not re-enter service until late 1976. Interestingly, neither of the latter two classes were ever based at Kingston Garage.

In the evening rush hour of 4 June 1975, Kingston RF480 leaves the British Aircraft Corporation's Weybridge factory, originally the Vickers' Works, bound for home on route 219. This route, along with the 218, would be the last to operate red RFs at the end of March 1979.

Not far away, modernised Green Line RF140 stands outside Addlestone Garage after a turn on route 462. A group of defunct SMs, which had replaced the last RLHs only in July 1970, may be seen dumped at the rear of the garage.

By the summer of 1975, London Transport had so many withdrawn MB-types in store that they ran out of garage space to house them. One answer was to dump them in any available space in Underground depots. Here, MBS259, MBS256 and MBS253 accompany a train of 1967 tube stock at the Victoria Line's Northumberland Park Depot on 7 June 1975. All three had recently been on loan to London Country, but with their seven-year certificates of fitness expiring in the summer, they never ran again. A few weeks later, London Transport rented space at the disused Radlett Airfield to store their defunct MBs, most of which eventually went for scrap in 1977.

During the summer of 1975, Palmers Green Garage was rebuilt with wider entrances and exits in order to accommodate DMSs. While this work was progressing, some of its allocation was outstationed at nearby Wood Green, where RT4613 heads a line-up of RTs in this former trolleybus depot, also on 7 June 1975.

Illustrating how many London Country routes that had RTs or RM-types on weekdays were now converted to one-person-operation on Sundays, Harlow RF302 heads through Thornwood Common on route 339 on 8 June 1975. A fairly new SNC-class Green Line coach follows on route 718.

On the same day, RT3321 is being prepared for a three-year repaint and recertification in Loughton Garage's large maintenance area. It had been off the road since February, and did not reappear in service until November. This was possibly because such work was often carried out by staff working overtime. The RT lasted its full three years, until November 1978. The MB beside it, one of Loughton's own allocation for route 20, is by now one of very few of this class still in service.

By this time, only two of the relatively few Night Bus routes then operating were still RT-operated, the N95 and the N98. On the latter, Seven Kings RT4728 passes through Holborn Circus in the early morning of 26 June 1975.

More usual by now was the use of DMs and DMSs on such routes. On the same day, Holloway DM1741 is seen in Procter Street, Bloomsbury, on route N92, successor of the night-tram service between the Embankment and Archway on route 35.

Seen approaching Bushey Arches on 10 July 1975, red MBS57 is one of several on loan to London Country at Garston Garage, working local route 346. It remained there until withdrawn at the end of the year.

Another MBS at Garston that day is MBS74, seen at the junction of Aldenham Road and Chalk Hill, Bushey. A standee MBS may have been acceptable on the local 346, but surely not on the long 335 from Watford to Windsor. This one was withdrawn in August.

Complete with a set of RML side blinds for its front via display, Garston RT994 is seen at St. Peter's Church, Bushey, on route 306, standing in for an RML which had replaced RTs on this route more than nine years previously. At this period so many of Garston's RMLs were off the road awaiting spare parts that routes 306 and 311 were virtually reverted to RT operation.

Seen on the stand outside the London Transport canteen in Allsop Place, alongside Baker Street Station, in the evening of 10 July 1975, Dorking RF122 works the new Green Line route 703, which had recently replaced the southern section of the 714 between here and Dorking. A clumsily-applied handwritten '703' has been stuck over '714' on its blind. This route was very short-lived, being introduced on 31 May 1975 and withdrawn in the spring of 1976. The 714 to Dorking was subsequently reintroduced but started at Victoria.

At this period, RMLs at Staines were off the road owing to shortage of spare parts, too. Once again RTs had to cover for them – RT3252 is seen on route 441 in Thorpe Road, Egham, on 11 July 1975. Note its masked via blind-box, so applied to fit an RML via blind.

In nearby Staines that day, locally-based modernised Green Line RF194 working route 469 in South Street still carries the early 1970s London Country symbol.

One of a number of traditional London Transport routes never to be RM operated daily was the 89, although following the conversion of routes 1 and 21 from RT to RM operation early in 1975, its Saturday allocation from New Cross Garage did convert to RM. On 12 July 1975, RM1066 is seen in Montpelier Road, Blackheath. This state of affairs continued until the 89's conversion to DMS OPO in April 1978.

In contrast to the red MBSs seen in Watford earlier, MB95 is actually one of London Country's own, and is seen at Bushey Arches on school route 346D on 16 July 1975. Based at Garston, it is one of a handful to have received an overhaul (in December 1974) and looks quite smart in corporate NBC green and white livery. It would survive in service until December 1978.

At Uxbridge Station the same day, RF418 on route 224 and RF398 on route 223 represent the RFs which had replaced RTs from Uxbridge Garage on these routes, as well as the 204 and 224B in January 1971.

Yet another London Country garage whose RMLs were falling by the wayside at this time was Windsor. As a result, RT2722 is working route 452 (recently renumbered from 457A) in place of an RML when seen passing the General Eliot pub beside the Grand Union Canal in Uxbridge. It too has a masked blind-box to fit RML via blinds.

One of the southern extremities of the London Transport system was Church Cobham, where Norbiton RF513 is seen terminating, also on 16 July 1975. By now, final replacement of the many RFs working in this area was in sight – though not until the following year.

On the evening of the same day, Camberwell RM2129 is seen working the 40's Saturday projection at East Ham, White Horse terminus flanked by two of the dreadful DMSs which cursed route 5 at this time.

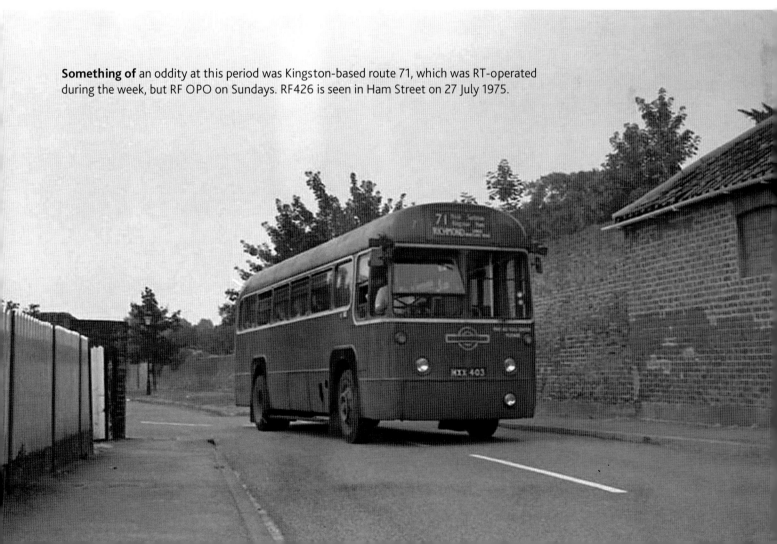

Something of an oddity at this period was Kingston-based route 71, which was RT-operated during the week, but RF OPO on Sundays. RF426 is seen in Ham Street on 27 July 1975.

Three types of London Transport OPO vehicles are seen in King Street, Twickenham, on 21 August 1975; Hounslow RF321 loads up on route 202 bound for Richmond, with DMS1350 and an SM following. No prizes for guessing which of the three was the most reliable!

A new London Transport class to appear during 1975 was the BS, small Bristol LHSs with ECW 26-seat bodywork. The first six entered service in August 1975, replacing Ford Transit minibuses on route C11 from Holloway Garage, whose BS4 is seen in Primrose Hill Road on 25 August 1975. A further eleven of this class followed replacing the remaining minibuses on routes B1, P4 and W9. This one is now preserved.

At Victoria, Eccleston Bridge on August Bank Holiday Monday, 25 August 1975, Windsor RF620 is given a well-earned drink when standing in for an RP on Green Line route 705. This was the last bank holiday when RFs were seen here in any significant numbers.

Having worked short to Feltham Station on route 237, Hounslow RF443 accompanies Fulwell SMS824 there on route 285 on 26 August 1975. The RF was later preserved.

A surprise at this period was the repainting in full NBC corporate green livery of London Country driver-training RT2230. It heads north up the Edgware Road through Burnt Oak on 27 August 1975 and was based at Harlow at the time.

Seen outside Potters Bar Station later the same day, the sole FRM1 awaits homegoing commuters on local route 284. Note the nasty dent between decks on its nearside front. However, this view shows quite clearly how much more attractive its bodywork is than that on the ugly DMSs.

On 28 August 1975, BEA Routemaster coach No.35 leaves The Queens Building at Heathrow Airport for the West London Air Terminal. By now, this was one of the last of these sixty-five coaches, which were operated and maintained for BEA by London Transport, to carry this orange and white livery and almost certainly the last in service, since the following day, along with twelve others, it was sold to London Transport.

Showing one of Palmers Green Garage's newly widened entrance/ exits, this view sees their RF419 setting off on route 212 for the trip around the North Circular road on 31 August 1975. The other RF is RF401, which now operates in conjunction with the Epping Ongar Railway on route 381 during the summer months.

Brand new on its first day of service, 1 September 1975, DM1126 from Wandsworth Garage has just replaced RTs on tram replacement route 168 when seen on Victoria Embankment. An RT on route 109 follows. Today, no London bus services run along this road which was once thronged with trams.

London Country had also bought ECW-bodied Bristol LHs for use on rural services, but here on 4 September 1975, Dunton Green BL5 has been pressed into service on Green Line route 705. It appears to be empty when crossing Lambeth Bridge.

On sister route 704 from the same garage, RF187 'also crossing Lambeth Bridge that day' proves that anything goes on London Country and Green Line services! This RF had been downgraded from Green Line coach to Country bus status upon overhaul in the mid-1960s, and remained in service until January 1976.

Somewhat unusually, Harlow Town Service 807 had rush hour journeys to and from Epping Station at this period. Harlow RT3315 calls at the Carpenters Arms, Thornwood Common, and is about to be overtaken by an RP on route 718 on 10 September 1975.

'**Beauty and** the Beast?' At Roehampton, Earl Spencer, Riverside RT2446 works a short journey on route 72 back to Hammersmith on 11 September 1975, whilst Putney DMS560 has also turned short there on route 85. RMs replaced the 72's RTs in December.

London Country
RCL2237 was unique in being the only one to bear NBC corporate livery and a Green Line fleet name, being one of the three kept at Godstone Garage for route 709. Here, however, it was working from Crawley Garage on the long 405 Country bus route when seen passing the Red Lion in Coulsdon, also on 11 September 1975.

On 13 September 1975, Hanwell RML2441 and Uxbridge RML2398 pass Ealing Town Hall on short workings of route 207 to Acton Vale. This route converted to crew DM a few weeks later, but these proved to be such a disaster that the 207 reverted to Routemaster operation in 1980, retaining them until the spring of 1987.

On 16 September 1975, freshly overhauled RM733 stands in for one of Cricklewood's crew DMs on route 16, as one of them follows it outside the Crown at Cricklewood Broadway. Having gained DMs in December 1973, the 16 also reverted to Routemaster operation in 1980.

A very unusual working indeed on 18 September 1975 is that of Riverside RT1641 on route 74B, which was scheduled for RMLs. It is seen outside the Victoria & Albert Museum.

RT3 424 from Chelsham Garage is one of many operating extras on route 410 between Bromley North Station and Biggin Hill for the Air Display on 20 September 1975. It is seen bringing spectators back from the event at the Mark Inn, Keston, with RCL2226 in pursuit.

To illustrate the extremes London Country were now having to go to in order to resolve their vehicle shortages, three Southdown 'Queen Mary' Northern Counties-bodied Leyland Titan PD3s were obtained to help out Godstone's ailing RML fleet. LS2, originally Southdown No.933 new in 1958, is seen in South Croydon High Street on 8 October 1975. They were operated for just over a year, still bearing Southdown's traditional green and cream livery.

The ex-Southdown PD3s were not the only 'foreign' Leylands working in the Croydon area that day. Also owing to vehicle shortages, London Transport's route 190 at South Croydon Garage was wholly converted from RM to Leyland PD3 Titan operation, using buses hired from Southend Corporation. Their No.346 is a very late example, built in 1967, with East Lancs bodywork. It is seen in London Road, Coulsdon, working a 'short' to the Red Lion.

The majority of the Southend PD3s at South Croydon dated from 1965 and had Massey bodywork. Typical of them is No.341 which turns into Marlpit Lane, Coulsdon.

Also to combat vehicle shortages, London Transport's route 175 at Romford, North Street Garage was converted from RT to Routemaster operation in early October, using the thirteen ex-British European Airways coaches that had been acquired at the end of August. These were given fleet numbers RMA1-13. The last of these, RMA13, is seen on 9 October 1975 in Rush Green Road, Romford. They were pressed into service still bearing BEA orange and white livery, but with BEA names painted out and LT bullseyes added. They were also given stencil holders for their running numbers, removed from withdrawn MBs.

An oddity with the RMAs is that they were not fitted with blind-boxes; instead, a slip-board inserted in the front nearside window was deemed sufficient. Perhaps this was because they were never intended to last very long in service – indeed, they were replaced in September 1976 by RTs and demoted to trainers or staff-buses. Yet, many years later, some *were* fitted with blinds – probably using those taken from withdrawn RMs. On 11 October 1975, RMA1 shows its slipboard in Dagenham, Heathway. Owing to the lack of blinds, and also the vehicles' non-standard colour, many passengers at first ignored them, thinking they were 'workmen's buses'! They were unpopular with crews too, since there was nowhere for the conductor to stand, nor did they have stanchions for conductors or passengers to hold on to.

Meanwhile, London's DMSs were becoming ever more troublesome. On 12 October 1975, DMS64, a survivor from the first conversions to this type, has for some reason been diverted along Essex Road when working route 271 from Holloway Garage. The nasty dents at the nearside front are typical of this type at the time.

In contrast, busy route 24 has just received brand new crew-operated DMs on 19 October 1975. An inspector has curtailed DM1156, much to the annoyance of intending passengers, outside South Africa House at Trafalgar Square, where for once at this period there are no demonstrators protesting about apartheid. Chalk Farm-operated route 24 had, of course, been the first to operate rear-engined, front entrance double-deckers in the shape of the XA class ten years before. The new DMs were not a success on the route; RMLs returned in the spring of 1979. Note how this new DM has a different headlamp arrangement to that of the earlier DMS seen above.

London Country still had many London Transport MB-types on loan as 1975 drew to a close. MB17, second of the production examples and originally a 'Red Arrow' vehicle, works school route 346D from Garston Garage when seen arriving at Queens School, Bushey, on 6 November 1975. It spent a year there until withdrawal in March 1976. Once again, it sports a nasty dent on its front offside.

Garston AN53 is seen turning at Queen's School on a school journey of route 385, which had received this type in replacement of RTs in July 1972.

Owing to Garston's ongoing shortage of RMLs, RT3636 works a school journey on route 346C, also at Queen's School. Quite why pupils are *arriving* there in the afternoon is a mystery, and the awful flared trousers they are wearing somehow epitomise the naff 1970s!

At Garston Garage the same afternoon, a very battered MBS59, a veteran of the 7 September 1968 'Reshaping Plan' changes at Wood Green, sets off for an evening rush hour turn on route 352. This is possibly its last day in service, as it was withdrawn in early November. An AN and an RML complete the picture.

As route 306 seen earlier, by this time Garston's route 311 had reverted entirely to RT-operation owing to the shortage of RMLs. RT3530 is seen at Shenley War Memorial setting off for Leavesden.

Also in Shenley that day, SMW13, one of a dozen Marshall-bodied AEC Swifts diverted to London Country from South Wales Transport in 1971, is seen working route 358 from St. Albans Garage. These vehicles remained in service until early 1981.

Also a St. Albans vehicle, country bus Leyland National SNB98 has been pressed into service on Green Line route 712, on which it has terminated in Buckingham Palace Road, Victoria, on 21 November 1975.

At this period, London Transport staff buses were still outstationed at London Country garages. RF314 and RF486 stand outside their Bell Street, Reigate, headquarters on 29 November 1975. RF314 is of note in that, firstly, it has two fog lamps, and, secondly, that it was recertified and returned to service at Kingston two years after this picture was taken, remaining there until the end.

Another red London Transport bus at Reigate that day is MBS46, on loan to London Country to cover for its defunct green fellows on their pioneer country route, the 447. It is seen at the Red Cross terminus. It moved to Crawley in January 1976, spending almost the whole of that year there before withdrawal.

London Country were now borrowing vehicles from other operators, too. Bournemouth Corporation 1965 Weymann-bodied Daimler Fleetline No.194 has just arrived at Leatherhead Garage on 29 November 1975 when seen in the company of AN119. Carrying Bournemouth's distinctive yellow livery, several of these buses were to be loaned to London Country until as late as the spring of 1978.

Outside the garage, AN24 is seen on a short working of the long route 408 to Effingham, just departing after changing driver. It was problems in maintaining these vehicles that led to the hire of the Bournemouth Fleetlines.

As the new year of 1976 began, problems with London Transport's DMSs were becoming ever worse, but on 3 January 1976, Edgware DMS674 is apparently fit and well when seen at the Crown, Borehamwood, on route 292.

London Country was still relying very much on its elderly RFs as the year opened. Recently repainted in light green with a yellow relief band, Grays modernised ex-Green Line RF88 is seen on the level crossing at Purfleet Station on local route 374 on 10 January 1976.

At first sight a view of newly-overhauled RTs in Aldenham Works, this picture actually shows newly-recertified and repainted RT1791, 2792 and 1312 in the former trolleybus depot at Hanwell, where they had been done, on 24 January 1976. For some reason, RT2792 was demoted to training duties in June and sold in September, but the other two saw a couple of years' more service.

Not so lucky is RT2525, which has been involved in a very nasty accident when working route 102 on the North Circular Road, where a large lorry collided almost head-on with it in Edmonton. It is seen in its home garage, Palmers Green on 25 January 1976 and, not surprisingly, went for scrap in April.

The new Brent Cross Shopping Centre opened at this time, and to serve it, a number of bus routes were diverted or extended there. In addition, a variation of the 16, numbered 16A, was introduced to serve it. On the first day, 31 January 1976, Cricklewood DM951 is seen in the new Brent Cross Bus Station.

By now, routes 176 and 176A were the only ones scheduled (Mondays to Fridays only) for RT operation through or to the West End and City respectively. On 25 February 1976, Walworth RT2629 accompanies Bow RML2286 on the stand at Willesden Garage. The last RTs on these routes were replaced by RMs at the end of March, but RT2629 was kept on as a trainer. When it was finally withdrawn in the summer of 1979, it was sold for preservation and I was one of its co-owners.

Although by now London Transport had given up on the dreadful MB class, a handful were resuscitated for use at Dalston Garage on route S2. MBS202 is seen at its Clapton Pond terminus on 28 February 1976. They lasted here for only three or four months, however, though one or two saw further use as Red Arrow vehicles.

Following their replacement by new Routemaster coaches in the winter of 1966/67, four of the Park Royal-bodied 'half-deck' AEC Regal IVs that had been operated and maintained for British European Airways by London Transport were bought by LT and converted to mobile uniform issue units. MLL727 became service vehicle 1466W and is seen at Tottenham Garage on 30 March 1976.

Tottenham Garage became the focus of attention again at this period (as it had at the end of 1973) when three unscheduled RTs were allocated there to cover for a shortage of RMs. One of these, RT2178, passes beneath the Kentish Town to Barking line at South Tottenham Station on 1 April 1976, working one-time XA-operated route 76. This allocation was the first of many of spare RTs to various garages to bolster the RM and RML fleet during the ensuing eighteen months.

On the same day, Grays RMC1471 and RMC1472 are seen at Ockendon Station working routes 370A and 373. A number of London Country RCLs and RMCs were kept here to operate various routes serving factories in the area at this time.

Also a Grays vehicle, AN117 loads up at Rainham Church in the evening rush hour of the same day on route 328.

Somewhat oddly, the RMAs were painted red at their former BEA operating base, the old Chiswick Tram Depot. Here on 4 April 1976, RMA13 has just been done, but has been mis-registered KGJ613D. It is really NMY656E, as seen earlier in this book. The fact that the RMAs were acquired from BEA (or later British Airways) in different batches meant that they were given fleetnumbers as and when acquired, so most did not have matching fleet and registration digits as almost all other Routemasters did, leading to such confusion. The other buses in this view are still with BA, in their dark blue and white livery.

Following the experimental use of Metro-Scania single-deckers, London Transport ordered 164 double-deckers of this type, delivery of which began in the winter of 1975/76. They were hoped to be a possible replacement for awful DMSs, and indeed looked much smarter with this new livery of red with white upper-deck window surrounds. However, they proved to be prone to chassis corrosion and were also very heavy on fuel. Here, MD25 is seen on test at Westminster Station on 6 April 1976.

To replace the awkward 167A between Chigwell and Abridge, route 235 was extended from Chigwell, but owing to its one-person-operated vehicles not being able to terminate there, was further extended to Theydon Bois, where the village green provided a convenient turning point. On the first day of this arrangement, 10 April 1976, Leyton MB664 – penultimate member of this unhappy class – stands at the green, complete with a brand new bus stop. This MB, along with other survivors at Leyton, was withdrawn in June. The extension to Theydon Bois lasted until March 1979.

On the same day, Romford North Street RF461 crosses the River Roding at Abridge on route 250. New BL-class ECW-bodied Bristol LHs took over a fortnight later. The 250 was withdrawn in January 1977, replaced by an extension of route 247 which meant that this ran all the way from Epping to Brentwood via Romford.

Green Line route 713 was operated by SNC Nationals at this time, but on Easter Monday, 19 April 1976, St Albans RP77 works its bank holiday extension to Whipsnade Zoo when seen at Golders Green Station.

Presumably by coincidence, two of the three unscheduled RTs allocated to Tottenham Garage, RT2178 and RT2964, are seen together at the Tottenham Hale Station terminus of route 41 on 26 April 1976. This route had converted from RTW to RM operation in February 1964 from this garage; RMs from West Ham having worked it since it was extended to Docklands in connection with trolleybus replacement four years previously.

The new MD class was used initially to replace RMs on crew-operated routes in South East London. First to convert were the 36 group of routes. Peckham MD3 passes the Green Man at Beckenham Hill Park on 28 April 1976 on a short working of the 36B to Downham Way. The 36, 36A and 36B reverted to RM operation early in 1980, with the MDs being redeployed on OPO services in the Woolwich area.

By 2 May 1976, virtually all of the few surviving London Transport MB-types were on Red Arrow services in Central London. These were often used on railway replacement services at weekends; here, Victoria Gillingham Street MBA606 is seen so employed at Blackfriars Station, complete with a nasty offside dent.

Seen in the village of Hythe End, near Staines, Uxbridge RF370 and RF418 pass on route 224 on 13 May 1976. This was the last day route 224 ran in this area, since it was cut back from Laleham to Poyle the following day, as part of London Transport's 'out-county' route cuts.

On the same day, Stevenage RP28 is seen at the Chertsey Bridge terminus of route 716, about to set off on the long journey to distant Hitchin. This was also the final day of this working – next day the 716A was renumbered 716, which therefore went to Woking rather than Chertsey.

14 May 1976 was the final day of Green Line route 709. On its very last journey up to Baker Street, the sole NBC Green Line liveried RCL, Godstone RCL2237, passes the Imperial War Museum in Kennington Road. Note the banner in the nearside front window.

Bournemouth Fleetlines were not the only buses from that fleet loaned to London Country. Here, Bournemouth Corporation 1967 Daimler Roadliner No.53 is seen working from Staines Garage on local route 460 on 15 May 1976.

In April 1976, what would be the very last new London Transport route introduced with RTs, the 217B, began running between Enfield Town and the new Greater London Council 'out-county' Ninefields North Estate, near Upshire. At the latter terminus, Ponders End RT3101 arrives on 23 May 1976. The route converted to DMS OMO in August 1977.

Another operator to which London Country turned to ease its vehicle shortage was Eastbourne Corporation, whose No 67, an East Lancs-bodied AEC Regent V new in 1963, stands in for a Swanley RMC on route 477 in Orpington High Street on 8 June 1976.

On the same day, modernised Green Line RF129, now demoted to bus status, stands in for an RP working route 704 from Dunton Green Garage at Farnborough Common. Note how the driver has its doors and all side windows open on what was one of the first scorching days of 1976's long, hot, dry summer.

One of the last red RFs to be overhauled, in the spring of 1973, Sutton RF485 is seen on route 80A on 11 June 1976 in Shelvers Way, Tadworth, just over two weeks before BLs replaced RFs here. It saw further service at Norbiton and Kingston garages before final withdrawal in January 1978.

Walthamstow RT1634 works one of the scheduled RT-operated journeys on otherwise RM-operated route 69 at Walthamstow Central Bus Station on 23 June 1976, as Loughton DMS1296 awaits departure for home on route 20 and another of the class follows on circular route W21.

Even in the very hot summer of 1976, it was unusual to see an RT with the driver's windows wide open, but they are on Leatherhead RT3450 working a Tadworth 'short' on route 406 on 3 July 1976 in Brook Street, Kingston. An SM on the 418 follows.

On the same day, a very well-laden Kingston RF527 passes through Hampton Village bound for Staines on route 216, which would convert to BL operation in September.

Another unscheduled operation at this time was of two RTs allocated to Clapton Garage, which covered for RM shortages on route 38. One of them, RT1161, is driven by Bert Barlow, my regular driver when I was a conductor at Clapton in 1974/75, at Islington, Angel, on 6 July 1976, as Tottenham RM1755 waits to turn right into Pentonville Road on route 73.

Modernised Green Line RF183, now demoted as most were by now to bus status, is seen on local route 469 in Clarence Street, Staines, its home town on 17 July 1976.

As a possible replacement for the awful DMS class, London Transport and British Leyland developed the Leyland B15 Titan. Here on 19 July 1976, the first prototype NHG732P is seen in trial service from Chalk Farm Garage on route 24 at Trafalgar Square, where it has been curtailed. Mass production of these buses began late in 1978, and they proved to be very successful. Of the 1,100 or so built, nearly all went to London Transport and some remained at London's service until the early 2000s.

The DMs based at Chalk Farm for the 24 worked their small share of route 3 on Sundays. On 25 July 1976, DM1142 turns from Crystal Palace Parade into College Road on its long journey home.

A bizarre unscheduled allocation of two RTs was made to Finchley Garage at the beginning of August 1976, and used to cover missing RMs on route 26 (New Barnet to Victoria via Golders Green), which had never been RT-operated before. One of them, RT4798, is seen at the foot of Park Lane on 4 August 1976.

Meanwhile, the hot summer of 1976 was causing havoc with the dreadful DMSs, whose engines kept overheating and often caught fire. This has happened to Wood Green DMS789 working route 221 at Manor House on 12 August 1976, requiring the attendance of the London Fire Brigade.

The leaves are already turning brown on 14 August 1976 owing to the hot dry summer, as Fulwell RF481 calls at Lower Green, Sandown Park, on route 206, which converted to BL operation eight days later. The famous Sandown Park racecourse is seen in the background.

On the same day, Red Arrow MBA608 is apparently being repainted by hand outside Norbiton Garage, and is presently in pink primer! It eventually re-entered service at Hackney Garage on route 502 in January 1977.

Also at the beginning of August 1976, six RTs appeared at Victoria, Gillingham Street Garage to cover for RMs on route 137. RTs had not operated from this garage for many years, though RTLs had done so until early 1967. RT2567 runs out for the evening rush hour on 16 August 1976.

Next day, 17 August 1976, also at Victoria, Clapton RT1706, which had been fully repainted and given a three-year recertification, provides an interesting contrast with one of the new MDs on route 36B in Grosvenor Gardens.

As mentioned earlier, route 224 had been cut back in May. The service usually ran from Uxbridge to Colnbrook, but there were rush hour extensions to the GAF factory at Poyle. Uxbridge RF427 is seen leaving there on 18 August 1976. This route had a massive upgrade from RF to DMS operation in December.

On sister route 224B the same day, Uxbridge RF364 arrives at its Stockley Estate, Mulberry Parade terminus. This route too gained DMSs four months later.

On a cloudless summer's day, Loughton RT3295 has just changed crew outside its garage on 21 August 1976. Route 20A converted to DMS OPO seven weeks later.

The Southend Corporation Leyland Titans PD3s were loaned to London Country after their stint at Croydon, replacing RTs from Harlow Garage on route 339. Also on 21 August 1976, Massey-bodied No.343 is about to do the route's double-run to Epping Station when seen passing LT DMS1665 on route 20 just north of Epping Town Centre. The Titans were replaced by London Country RMLs in January 1977.

By the late summer of 1976, RTs on Green Line routes had become a rarity, but Tring RT3530 was still a regular performer in evening rush hours on route 706, and is seen here at Marble Arch on Friday, 3 September 1976.

Finchley's second RT for route 26, RT2143, had a three-year recertification and repaint, so looks very smart when loading up at Golders Green War Memorial on 18 September 1976. The hand-drawn number blind, with no via points, made the two RTs on this route look quite odd, and they were there for over a year.

Edgware RF504 has lost the top half of its 'bullseye' filler-cap cover when seen in Oakleigh Road South, New Southgate, on 9 October 1976. Route 251 converted to BL at the end of January 1977, but after nearly a year in store, this RF was recertified in January 1978 and sent to Kingston, where it remained until the end.

Fortunately, at least when London Transport drivers were trained at the famous Chiswick Works, accidents involving London buses were rare. However, during the night of 11/12 October 1976, when working Night Route N83, Stamford Hill RML2711 mounted the pavement in Fleet Street and demolished the front of an estate agent's shop, apparently as its driver had collapsed at the wheel. I encountered the spectacle seen here of it being extracted from the shop front on my way to 'work' at County Hall.

Seen just south of Palmers Green Triangle, not far from my present home, Palmers Green RT2775 stands in for an RM on route 298 on 16 October 1976. This RT had been on a tour to North America when new in 1952, and always retained its original body. It is now preserved.

Still in Green Line livery, St. Albans RF168 is seen in its home town in St. Peters Street, also on 16 October 1976, working route 313 to Enfield. This route has subsequently become a London Buses service, running from Potters Bar to Chingford via Enfield.

I was in for a shock when riding on a DM on route 29 from home at Wood Green to Westminster on my way to 'work' at County Hall on the morning of 4 November 1976, when I passed an RT heading the other way on route 141. This was another unscheduled allocation, this time to help RM shortages at Wood Green Garage. Needless to say, I alighted from the DM to wait for the RT to return southwards. It was RT2506, which had been reinstated from training duties after six years. This view shows it arriving at Moorgate, Finsbury Square, and it was one of two on the 141. I was very late for 'work' that morning and of course blamed the buses!

Holloway Garage also gained a number of unscheduled RTs at this time, which worked on all of its RM and RML-operated routes. Smartly repainted, RT3911 is seen passing Green Park on the 19 on 8 November 1976.

Holloway's RTs even occasionally stood in for the awful crew DMs on route 29. RT2352 contrasts with Battersea DMS578 on route 39 in Victoria Street on 11 November 1976. The 29 had received DMs in December 1975.

At this same time, a batch of RTs was also sent to Putney, Chelverton Road Garage to help it with RM and RML shortages. These came from Thornton Heath Garage upon the completion of route 109's long-drawn-out conversion to RM, and a shabby RT2812 still shows its TH garage code when working route 30 at Hyde Park Corner on 15 November 1976. RTs had last been allocated to this route in 1955, when the last wartime 2RT2s were withdrawn.

Even more drastic was the conversion of the whole of route 230 from RM to RT operation at Leyton Garage at the beginning of December. This route had never been RT operated, having been introduced in June 1973, and Leyton had lost their last RTs at the end of October 1972. RT3629 turns from Forest Road into Blackhorse Road, Walthamstow, on 11 December 1976. Note the special masking on the via blind to fit RM blinds.

Also still showing TH garage codes, Putney RT4363 is seen on the normally RML-operated route 74 in Knightsbridge on 17 January 1977.

Many of the routes on which the spare RTs operated passed through the West End, thus it was possible to see them together on different routes. This has happened on 25 January 1977 as Victoria RT2602, an extra one added to those allocated the previous August, passes Putney RT4363 at the western end of Oxford Street. For some reason it has an RM rear number blind in its via box, rather than a side blind, giving the odd effect seen here.

Route 298 had been introduced in September 1968 to replace the northern end of the 29, originally venturing no further south than Turnpike Lane Station. In January 1970, it was revised and extended to Finsbury Park, but was cut back again in June 1973. Two years later, however, the extension was restored and on 26 February 1977, Palmers Green RM2123 escorts an RP on Green Line route 715 at Manor House. The extension was finally withdrawn three weeks after this picture was taken.

At this period, route 29 was extended on Sundays from Wood Green to Southgate Station, where Wood Green DM1181 stands on 6 March 1977. This was the penultimate Sunday of this working, since from 19 March, the 29 was rerouted and extended daily to Enfield Town via Palmers Green and Winchmore Hill. The 'offside' loading here is of note, something that would never be tolerated today.

In the evening of 18 March 1977, the second spare RT at Wood Green Garage, nicely repainted RT280, is seen amid a pack of DMSs having turned short on route 141 at Turnpike Lane Station. Next day, the RMs on this route were swopped with the DMs on route 29, to which the RTs also moved.

To commemorate Queen Elizabeth II's Silver Jubilee, twenty-five RMs were overhauled in a special silver livery, and renumbered SRM1-25. On Easter Sunday, 10 April 1977, they were launched at Battersea Park and toured Central London afterwards. Here, SRM17, alias RM1894, is seen with some of its fellows approaching Vauxhall Station on Albert Embankment.

Later the same day, Staines modernised Green Line RF183 is seen working route 718 at Victoria, having for some reason been fully repainted in London Country bus livery. Very few RFs now could be seen in such use, and despite the repaint, this one was withdrawn in January 1978.

The extension of route 29 saw it gain an additional daily RM allocation from Palmers Green Garage, alongside the existing ones from Holloway and Wood Green. Their RT3410 has stood in for an RM on 12 April 1977, and is seen here arriving at its terminus, Mornington Crescent Station, with Holloway RM420 following, going through to Victoria. These two buses took me on my journey to 'work' that morning.

Hounslow RF508 passes beneath the railway bridge in Heath Road, Twickenham, with an RM on route 281 in pursuit on 13 April 1977. Route 202 converted to BL five days later.

On the same day, RF517, also a Hounslow bus, is seen at Sunbury Church on a short working of route 237 to Feltham Station. This route too converted to BL on 18 April, leaving routes 218 and 219 at Kingston as the last London Transport routes to be operated by RFs.

Since there were only 25 SRMs, it was relatively unusual to catch two or more together in service. This lucky shot shows Bow SRM7 (RM1871) on route 25 passing Leyton SRM15 (RM1903) on route 38 at Green Park on 15 April 1977. Each SRM was sponsored by a different advertiser, and the buses were each transferred to a different garage twice during the year. They were repainted red in November and December 1977.

Some of the spare RTs helping out with RM and RML shortages were very shabby indeed. RT2052 has not had a fresh coat of paint for nearly ten years when seen on the Tottenham Court Road stand of route 14 on 22 April 1977. Being based at the huge Holloway Garage no doubt did not enhance its appearance, either!

Seen at the traffic lights at the junction of Whitehall and Charing Cross, RT3871 has just been allocated to Dalston Garage as a spare and makes its one and only appearance standing in for an RM on the busy route 11 on 2 May 1977. By a remarkable coincidence, this RT survived into preservation and is now part of the London Bus Company's Heritage Fleet and could be found working route 11 on a special running day in November 2014.

Though replaced by BSs on London Transport's first four minibus routes, some of the FS class Ford Transits survived to see further use on new route H2, linking the select back streets of Hampstead Garden Suburb with Golders Green Station. FS5 passes the Jewish cemetery in Hoop Lane on 7 May 1977.

By 12 May 1977, many Green Line routes had been drastically cut back, not least the 718 whose northern section had now been altered to run only from Walthamstow to Harlow, but also extended to Bishops Stortford to replace the withdrawn 720 and thus renumbered 702. The route should have been RP-operated, but was often instead worked by RMLs allocated to Harlow Garage for route 339. Here, a very shabby RML2352, which does not even show a route number, leaves Walthamstow Central Bus Station.

RFs were becoming very rare on Green Line work by this time, but also on 12 May 1977, Dartford NBC-liveried country bus RF690 is seen on the southern peripheral route 725 at Sidcup Station. An RT on route 228 and an RM on route 51A bring up the rear.

On the same day, Bexleyheath RT3480 has worked an afternoon school short journey to St. Mary Cray Station, and is seen on the stand awaiting departure on another short journey to Abbey Wood. Route 229 had been greatly extended in March 1959 to replace trolleybus route 698 between Bexleyheath and Woolwich, but on 21 May 1977, was withdrawn north of Erith and converted to RM operation.

Palmers Green RT2068 passes beneath the Piccadilly Line bridge at the junction of Hampden Way and Waterfall Road, Arnos Park, on local route 261 on 16 May 1977. The graffiti on the bridge reflects the political mood of the time – three weeks beforehand, the National Front had caused outrage by conducting a St. George's Day match through this predominantly Jewish area of London on what was also the Passover sabbath.

A very shabby Walthamstow RT2812 on route 34 escorts DMS798 from the same garage on route 144 along the North Circular Road at Edmonton, Regal, on 17 May 1977. The 34 converted to DMS OPO in September, but still runs today between Barnet and Walthamstow. On the other hand, the 144 no longer heads east from Edmonton, instead turning north up Fore Street and terminating at Edmonton Green.

One of the shortest-lived RM operations in London Transport's history was that of route 51A, which only lasted from January to May 1977. On 17 May 1977, three days before the route was withdrawn, Sidcup RM682 turns from Willersley Avenue into Halfway Street, Sidcup.

Kingston was always associated with red RFs, needed owing to the many very low bridges on routes worked in the area, so it is fitting that the last in London Transport's fleet were based there. These were allocated for routes 218 and 219, which were deemed too busy for conversion to BL, but could not be converted to the larger LS class Leyland Nationals as Kingston Garage was too small to accommodate them. From early 1977 onwards, RFs began to be recertified to keep services going here. One of the first was RF381, seen sporting the solid white roundel livery that RFs had not previously carried, when leaving Kingston Bus Station on a 218 short to Esher on 18 May 1977.

Illustrating how their forward staircases were removed to accommodate an instructor's seat behind the driver on those converted for training duties, West Ham RMA4 is seen so employed in Lordship Lane, Wood Green, on 20 May 1977. Also visible is the canopy route number box briefly used when it was in service on route 175.

At Carterhatch Lane terminus on 24 May 1977, Ponders End RM2210 unusually works local route 135 instead of an RT, although the route did gain RMs in January 1978. It accompanies DMS1425 from the same garage working route 231.

At Aldenham Works on 26 May 1977, newly overhauled RM700 carries one of the early bodies built in 1959/60 with non-opening front upper-deck windows. These were now up to eighteen years old, and receiving their third full overhauls, thus illustrating London Transport's faith in their Routemasters. A newly delivered DMS, with the much improved livery including white upper-deck window surrounds, stands behind.

On the same occasion, DMS2003 and DMS1976 illustrate how flimsy the bodywork on these ridiculous contraptions was. Both had been involved in collisions, but both were rebuilt and saw further service into the 1980s. The RM on the far left is newly-overhauled and awaiting painting.

A second new Green Line route based at Harlow was the 703, also replacing the 720 between Bishops Stortford, Harlow and Epping and then creating a new link to Waltham Cross. On 28 May 1977, Harlow RP15 loads up at Waltham Abbey. RMLs often covered for defunct RPs on this route, too.

Busy route 370, from Tilbury Ferry to Romford, was by now the preserve of RMCs and RCLs from Grays Garage. On 30 May 1977, RCL2237 passes beneath Upminster Bridge Station a few days before new ECW-bodied Bristol VRs of the BT class replaced the Routemasters on this service.

A very surprising move at this time was the repainting of three London Country RTs in full, corporate NBC light green livery. They were sent to Chelsham Garage, by now the last stronghold of the class. RT1018 passes beneath the bridge at Upper Warlingham Station on 1 June 1977, working local route 453. Sadly, they would only last a few months in service.

At the same garage, a batch of 1967 Massey-bodied Leyland Atlanteans was on loan from Maidstone Corporation, in whose light blue and cream livery No.35 looks very shabby when seen passing beneath the Brighton main line in Sussex Road, South Croydon, on route 403 also on 1 June 1977.

This was Derby Day, and at Epsom Station, Grays RCL2245 is one of several sent to Leatherhead Garage for the day to work racegoers' route 406F. Behind it is one of the three NBC-liveried RTs, Chelsham's RT3461. This was the last time ex-London Transport vehicles dominated the Derby Day services.

Peculiarly, four RTs were loaned to Sutton Garage on Derby Day to work extras on route 164A (which served Tattenham Corner), which had converted from RT to RM operation in January. One was Plumstead RT3365, which has turned short at St. Helier, Rose, and is seen here with its 'unofficial' conductor – me, who 'gave the real conductor the bell' leaving him free to collect fares. I had left my brief spell of work as a conductor with London Transport some two years previously, so this was rather naughty of me.

On 3 June 1977, Harlow RMLs 2311 and 2350 have done their double-runs through Epping town centre to and from the station, and are seen at Epping Parish Church. RMLs worked this route for only a few months, before being replaced by OPO vehicles.

Brand new London Country Leyland National SNB268 has just entered service at Reigate Garage, where it will stay for only a few days, when seen down the 'Dilly on Green Line route 711 on 16 June 1977. These vehicles were by now rapidly ousting surviving RFs, as well as MBs and SMs and London Country's Routemasters too. One of London Transport's MD-class Metro-Scanias follows on route 53, based at New Cross. Route 711, then still running throughout from High Wycombe to Reigate, was withdrawn in 1978.

The MDs based at New Cross for the 53 strayed on rare occasions to route 141, which was DM-operated from the garage. This has happened on 21 June 1977, as MD139 passes the Mildmay Tavern, where the pop group the Honeycombs, who provided Joe Meek with his last No.1 hit record, *Have I The Right?* in 1964, were supposedly 'discovered'. The conductress, complete with her trusty Gibson ticket machine, shows that the MD is crew-operated, as they all were at first.

London Country's Routemasters (of all three types – RMC, RCL and RML) were rapidly being replaced by OPO vehicles. On 28 June 1977, Crawley RCL2256 hurries along High Street, South Croydon, shortly before this fate befell trunk route 405. This view clearly shows the RCL's rear platform doors. After it had become a red bus in 1980, this one was involved in a rear-end accident and was rebuilt with a standard RM/RML open platform in 1981. It was therefore unique and survives today.

On 6 July 1977, the two 'rogue' RTs helping out at Wood Green Garage on route 29 were for some reason loaned to nearby Palmers Green Garage for the day. One of them, RT2506, has just run in after the evening rush hour and accompanies SMS545, one of those which had replaced RFs on route 212 in the spring of 1976. This SMS was one of few to have an overhaul at Aldenham (early in 1978) but even then was withdrawn at the end of 1980. Meanwhile, at this period, Palmers Green still operated three routes with RTs – the 34, 102 and 261, although the 34 converted to DMS OPO early in September. The RT seen here survived in service until the spring of 1978, ending up at Catford Garage.

For some reason, Silver Jubilee SRM23 (RM1902) is one of two that came to County Hall for a civic reception on 8 July 1977. It is seen in the 'inner sanctum' of the Members' car park; the steps and door behind the RM lead to the Council Chamber. This picture is completely unique – I took it from the window of the gents' lavatory on the ground floor, somewhere that only a GLC employee like myself could access!

A very strange vehicle operating in London at this time was former Leeds Corporation 1959 Roe-bodied Daimler CVG6 7517UA, painted red and hired to London Transport to test various new features which eventually led to the production of Dennis Dominator buses. It was based at Turnham Green Garage and worked route 27, on which it is seen on 15 July 1977 in Queensway.

By 20 July 1977, several London Country Routemasters had succumbed to the vehicle spares shortage and been stripped of such mechanical (and body) parts they still had to keep others in service. They were now redundant, too, and many were dumped at Grays Garage. This view shows RCL2227, RML2420 and RML2426 fronting a group of others. Ironically, all three carry NBC corporate livery yet the latter had not run in service since December 1973. Sadly, they were sold for scrap at the end of the year, supposedly with the scrap dealer (Wombwell Diesels) returning usable parts to London Transport.

Barking RT678 arrives at Dagenham Dock on route 148 in the evening rush hour of 22 July 1977, as another RT sets off on route 139 for Ilford. Both routes converted to DMS OPO next day.

At scenic Waltham Abbey on 16 August 1977 newly-overhauled RM217 works eponymous route 217 from Ponders End Garage. The garage was by now short of serviceable RTs, and routes 217 and 217B were to convert to DMS OPO just four days later. Until the latter route was introduced in April 1976, Ponders End RMs could not work their RT-operated routes (and vice-versa) owing to not having the relevant blinds, but all RTs and RMs there were fitted with sets to cover all their crew routes when they had to be changed to accommodate the new route.

Another real oddity working the same day is Hertford RML2347, seen at the roundabout at the junction of the Great Cambridge Road and Bullsmoor Lane on route 316. This route had been introduced as a one-man-operated service, and RMLs had never been scheduled to operate from Hertford Garage, either. Such was London Country's desperate vehicle shortage now that any roadworthy vehicles were sent to help out at whatever garages needed them; this RML had been sent to Hertford in July, remaining there until November when it was withdrawn. The following month, it was sold to London Transport.

By 7 September 1977, a new southern peripheral Green Line route, the 726, had been introduced as a variant of the 725. Windsor RP73 is a long way from home when seen in Long Lane, Beckenham. By now, this class was falling by the wayside.

On the last day of RT operation on route 34, 9 September 1977, Walthamstow RT3748 is seen at Leyton Green in the company of Leyton SRM19 (RM1904) which lays over before returning south on route 38. The SRMs too will soon be a memory; all were painted red and reverted to their normal stocknumbers by the end of the year.

The last new allocation of unscheduled RTs to be made to cover for RM shortages was of two of them to Camberwell Garage. Both came from Walthamstow following route 34's DMS conversion on 10 September 1977. As far as is known, only one actually ran on just the one occasion – this was RT1152, of which I was very lucky to catch this shot in Shoreditch High Street in the evening rush hour of 15 September 1977, working route 35. A few days later, both were transferred to Catford Garage.

On 24 September 1977, Staines RML2453 stands at the entrance to its home garage having worked local route 469. Behind it may be seen RML2449, which had been off the road for two years, and was another to go for scrap at the end of the year.

South-East London was still nicknamed 'RT Land' as Catford RT2788 lays over at Beckenham Junction Station on 27 September 1977, having disgorged a group of schoolchildren. This route, along with the 89 and 122 in the same area, finally lost its RTs in April 1978 (to DMS OPO) though route 94 retained them until the end of August that year – the last RT route in 'RT Land'.

By 28 September 1977, most unscheduled RT allocations had ceased, as the vehicle spares situation finally improved for London Transport. However, Holloway RT2352 was quite remarkably pressed into service on crew DM-operated route 104 in the evening rush hour that day. I just missed it at Archway Station, and nearly gave myself a seizure chasing it down Holloway Road. Fortunately, for once a DMS did me a favour in that I was able to beat the RT to its Moorgate terminus by riding on one there on the shorter and quicker 271 route! It is seen at Finsbury Square awaiting return to North Finchley. A very battered DM from the same garage stands behind on route 214.

On 30 September 1977, Windsor RML2454 is seen in Slough Town Centre on local route 407, as an MBS follows. This route would be one of the last outposts of London Country RML operation, surviving into 1980.

At route 150's remote Lambourne End terminus, newly-overhauled RM802 arrives on 14 October 1977, the last day London buses ran there. This was the only day RMs ever reached Lambourne End, since it was also the last day of crew operation on the normally RT-operated route, and the last day of RTs at Seven Kings Garage which operated it. RMs were used on that day to facilitate the transfer away of the RTs.

Cross-country routes 330 and 341 were the last in the former northern Country Area to be RMC operated. On 18 October 1977, St. Albans RMC1498 passes through the Hertfordshire village of Fleetville shortly before Leyland Nationals took over both routes.

From the same garage, ex-South Wales Transport AEC Swift SMW10 is seen in Hatfield Road, Oaklands, on the same day. The days of these vehicles were numbered, too.

By 20 October 1977, most of the spare RTs allocated to various garages to help cover for RM shortages had moved away, the last of all leaving Holloway Garage in December. Here, their RT3911 stands in for an RML on route 14 at a rainy King's Cross.

The last RMCs allocated to the former northern Country Area were on route 341. Hatfield RMC1512 passes through the village of Smallford on 10 November 1977, two days before replacement by Leyland Nationals. This RMC would be the last one in London Country service in February 1980.

Seen at Aldenham Works also on 10 November 1977, a batch of Bournemouth Corporation 1965 Weymann-bodied Daimler Fleetlines has just been acquired by London Transport for its Round London Sightseeing Tour. They had detachable tops, and became LT's seven-strong DMO class. Bournemouth No.187, nearest the camera, became DMO6 and has subsequently been preserved.

A rarely seen London Transport service vehicle is 1492B, a 1967 Bedford ambulance stationed at Aldenham Works. Obviously, this large establishment needed first aid facilities, and the vehicle is seen in its own ambulance bay. Note how its registration number is in the same series as the last batch of RMLs.

This view of a gutted SMS368 dumped in Poplar Garage on 1 January 1978 nicely illustrates the sad fate of most of this unfortunate class. Next to it, DMS1585 is also out of action, but will eventually be returned to service and last until October 1980.

Palmers Green RT3 410 is boiling over when seen on route 102 at Muswell Hill on 4 January 1978. Its driver has had to pull in to the bus stand and bring a watering can to the rescue! This route was gradually converted to RM operation over the following few weeks.

Seen at Leatherhead Garage on 21 January 1978, modernised Green Line RF79 is being converted to a towing vehicle, involving cutting away part of its rear end. It has a new livery of grey and yellow.

In **Leatherhead** town centre the same day, RT981 is seen running back to the garage from route 406. By now, this was one of only two London Country RTs still in service, and the last in the old Lincoln green livery. It was demoted to training duties in February, and subsequently preserved.

In December 1977, the inevitable happened – London Country Routemasters began to be bought back by London Transport. At first, RMCs and RCLs were used as driver trainers, still in green livery, often releasing RTs in that role back into service. RCL2223 is seen in Lordship Lane, Wood Green, on 25 January 1978. Some of the RMLs acquired were pressed into service with just a repaint into red, though most were sent to Aldenham for overhaul. A few of these were initially used as trainers, too.

A very strange alteration at the end of January 1978 was the conversion of route 237 from BL (which it had been since they replaced RFs in April 1977) to RM operation. At the same time, the route was cut back from Chertsey to Sunbury Village, and extended from Hounslow to Shepherd's Bush replacing route 117. On the last day of BL operation, 27 January 1978, Hounslow BL87 is seen passing the Bell in Hounslow.

Following its second overhaul, the solitary FRM1 was sent to Stockwell Garage to work the Round London Sightseeing Tour, on which it is seen at Monument Station on 16 February 1978.

Also at Monument that day, ex-London Country trainer RMC1497, now based at Brixton, shows how these vehicles were now given LT bullseyes whilst retaining green livery.

A number of SMSs were altered in 1976/77 to become the SMD class, which entailed sealing up their centre doors and giving them extra seats. This is the hulk of SMD59, which lasted only a few months in this form before being withdrawn. Here it is dumped in Kingston coal yard on 17 February 1978 shortly before sale for scrap. Behind is RF363, which languished there for the rest of the year, being cannibalised for spare parts to keep the survivors at Kingston in service.

At route 71's Richmond, Dee Road terminus later the same day, Kingston RT1654 sets off for Chessington Zoo. Beside it, freshly overhauled RM1991 has just come from Aldenham and been pressed into service for the evening rush hour. RMs gradually replaced route 71's RTs over the next three weeks.

RM1128 looks very sorry for itself when seen stored in Bexleyheath Garage – which ironically would never operate its own Routemasters – on 4 March 1978. It had fallen victim to the vehicle spares shortage in May 1975 when based at Stockwell Garage and was gradually robbed of body and mechanical parts to keep its fellows in service. At the time this picture was taken, there were fears that this RM, and three or four others similarly disabled around the fleet, would be scrapped, but in the event, all were eventually repaired. This one would re-enter service in September 1979.

By now, the busy route 480 running between Erith and Gravesend was the last major London Country route allocated RMLs. They were becoming very shabby too, as Northfleet RML2338, in very faded Lincoln green livery, shows when seen at Greenhithe, also on 4 March 1978.

London Transport's RTs were still being recertified at this period, though now not usually repainted. Something of a surprise, therefore, was to find RT2750 being fully repainted in West Ham Garage on 7 March 1978. As may be seen, it had been on training duties. It re-entered service at Barking later in the month, though curiously was demoted to staff bus duties at the end of October when route 87 converted to RM operation.

One of the former London Country RMLs which was merely repainted red when acquired by London Transport was RML2332. As may be seen, its dented front dome was not even repaired. It passes the police station in Dalston Lane on 8 March 1978 working route 48 from Leyton Garage. When it was overhauled in 1979, it was one of few ex-London Country RMLs to change bodies.

The last garage to operate RTs in North London was Palmers Green, where they were gradually replaced by RMs on routes 102 and 261 between January and March 1978. On 29 March 1978, the last one of all, RT3754, awaits departure from the garage on route 102 for the evening rush hour. It was withdrawn two days later.

Representing ex-London Country RMLs which received full overhauls at Aldenham before entering service as red buses, RML2317 sets off from Hendon Garage for route 13 on 7 April 1978.

A fortnight before the circuitous South East London route 122 converted to RM operation, Plumstead RT786 is seen at its Slade Green Station terminus, to where it was extended on Saturdays from Bexleyheath, on 8 April 1978. It is accompanied by Bexleyheath DMS21, fresh from an Aldenham overhaul which had taken six months, rather than the usual one month for such types as RFs, RTs and RMs.

Another RT-operated route in South-East London which lost them on 22 April 1978 was the 146, operated by Bromley Garage and serving the rural village of Downe. Difficult turning arrangements there had forestalled its conversion to one-man operation, although eventually it was found BLs could work there. RT3202 is seen out in the wilds in Rookery Road, between Keston and Downe, also on 8 April 1978.

Shortages of serviceable RTs at this time meant more were returned to service from driver training duties, in turn causing a shortage of training buses. As a result, London Transport had to resort to hiring preserved RTs for the purpose. Here, Saunders-bodied RT1320 has just left Chiswick Works on 11 April 1978. The vehicle is restored in 1948 Country Area green livery, yet no Saunders-bodied RT was ever green in colour.

On the same occasion, London Transport's first Metrobus, then numbered MT1, is also seen at Chiswick Works shortly after delivery. Later renumbered M1, it was one of five that entered trial service at Cricklewood Garage later in the year. Full production of the type began in September 1978, and they began to replace DMSs six months later. Unlike those awful things, they proved to be very successful. More than 1,400 were built for London Transport, many seeing more than twenty years' service.

Bexleyheath RT3949 climbs steep Shooters Hill on the horseshoe-shaped route 89, which ran from Lewisham to Eltham via Welling, Bexley and Blackfen on 14 April 1978. This was the last route to operate RTs at the garage, converting to DMS OPO eight days later.

In the same area, Godstone-operated route 410 had been converted to OMO AF-class Daimler Fleetlines early in 1972, but problems with this small class of eleven buses which had been diverted from Western Welsh meant that RMLs based there for the 409 often still had to be used. This has happened as RML2334 crosses Keston Common on a short working to Biggin Hill, also on 14 April 1978.

Not far away, on 16 April 1978, Bromley RM399 is seen in New Road Hill, approaching the village of Downe. Route 146 was allocated one RM on Sundays, and this was the last day of this operation – the bus has a special slipboard marking the event, and most of its passengers are enthusiasts.

Hanwell SMS668 has disgraced itself by breaking down whilst working route E3 in Southfield Road, Acton, and in the process blocking the road in both directions; another SMS is stranded behind it, as were two others heading in the opposite direction! The date is 17 April 1978. Such happenings were typical of this dreadful class; this one never ran again and was withdrawn in May 1978, when it would have been due for its first overhaul. New Leyland Nationals replaced SMSs on route E3 in September.

On 18 April 1978, Palmers Green RM236 climbs Waterfall Road, New Southgate, on route 261, which was unofficially converted from RT to RM operation at this period. It received OPO DMSs four days after this picture was taken.

Things are not what they seem in this view of London Country RT4743 leaving Chiswick Works on training duties on 19 April 1978. It had in fact been sold by LCBS in January 1977, and subsequently preserved. Here, it is on loan to London Transport to cover the shortage of trainers. It was later exported to Canada and used on tour work there.

London Country's last RT in service, NBC-liveried RT604, survived even after LCBS' RM-types had begun to be sold. It is seen, curiously minus a number blind display, working route 403 from Chelsham Garage at Fairfield Halls, East Croydon, also on 19 April 1978. When it was finally withdrawn in September, it was rescued for preservation and is a regular performer at vintage bus running days almost forty years later.

The replacement of RTs on routes 89, 122 and 146 on 22 April 1978, removed all but those working route 94 in South East London from what had been called 'RT Land'. Three of them, headed by RT1791, are seen that day leaving the Woolwich Ferry, heading for the RTs' final stronghold – Barking. This one, however, only lasted there until route 87's conversion to RM at the end of October.

By this period, the former Clapham Bus Garage, which had been closed amid the 1958 service cuts and then used as the Museum of British Transport until 1973, had been repossessed by London Transport for use as a store for new or withdrawn vehicles. On 24 April 1978, withdrawn SM-types predominate, with SMD393 nearest the camera. An MS and a DMS may also be seen. The two Routemasters in the background are RCLs recently re-acquired from London Country. Unlike most of its fellows, the SMD was sold for further use and exported to Algeria! Clapham Garage was reopened operationally in 1981, remaining so until 1987 covering for rebuilding work at nearby Norwood and Streatham garages.

Seen later the same day, Chelsham RCL2249 departs for home from route 403's Wallington Station terminus. This was by now the last stronghold of this class in London Country service; the last ones left there in December 1978.

By now, London Country were buying more Leyland Atlanteans. Also on 24 April 1978, brand new AN128 changes drivers in Leatherhead town centre.

At the end of April 1978, route 105 (worked from Southall and Shepherd's Bush Garages) converted from RT to RM operation. On the RTs' last day at the latter garage, RT837 has been put out on normally RML-operated route 88 – perhaps for the benefit of enthusiasts – on 29 April 1978, and I was lucky to catch it here just about to terminate at Shepherd's Bush Garage on its final run.

Quite surprisingly, Barking RTs still worked night routes N95 and N98 at this late stage. Here, their RT778 is seen early in the morning of 4 May 1978 at the junction of Goodmayes Lane and Longbridge Road on the last run back to the garage. Both routes converted to DMS, but with conductors, three weeks later.

One of the ex-Bournemouth Daimler Fleetlines bought for the Round London Sightseeing Tour, DMO2 looks very smart in open-top mode when seen about to cross London Bridge on 11 May 1978. They were based at Stockwell Garage.

By 27 May 1978, more Routemaster coaches had been acquired from British Airways. No.53 has become RMA25 and still carries full BA livery when seen in staff bus use at Harrow Weald Garage in the company of RT4779, one of their allocation for route 140.

London Country RC13, seen on training duties in Southborough Lane, Bromley, in 1 June 1978, is now one of just three of this type left in use. It is based at Northfleet Garage and will be withdrawn in September.

One of the most remarkable vehicles to be loaned back to London Transport for driver training was RTL525, seen here leaving Chiswick Works on 14 July 1978. The reason it has a 'P' registration is that it had been exported to Jersey after withdrawal by LT in 1959, and lost its original registration. This could not be regained when it returned to the mainland in 1976, presumably owing to the legacy of the Aldenham overhaul system.

Few Routemaster coaches now remained in use by British Airways, but here No.55 is one of two seen in Chiswick High Road, running out from the former Chiswick Tram Depot, also on 14 July 1978. All were bought by London Transport when the BA coach service was finally withdrawn at the end of March 1979.

Route 140 finally converted to RM operation on 15 July 1978, sixteen years after it should have done. The last RT to operate it, RT3234, runs out of Harrow Weald Garage for the final run on the evening of Friday, 14 July 1978, suitably decorated. The Union Flag has been lent by the National Front prospective parliamentary candidate for Watford, who was a transport enthusiast.

The last RT-operated route in South London was the 94, operated by Catford and Bromley Garages. On 26 July 1978, Catford RT280 passes one of its fellows in Franks Wood Avenue, Petts Wood, a month before the route's conversion to RM operation.

The RTs allocated for route 94 still strayed on to RM-operated routes 1, 47 and 119 right until the end. On 17 August 1978, just a week before, Bromley RT714 is seen on the latter route in Monks Orchard Road, Shirley.

The days of crew operation at Chelsham on route 403 were drawing to a close now, too. On 23 August 1978, RMC1479 sets off for West Croydon from Warlingham Park Hospital. Although this RMC was eventually sold back to London Transport, it never saw further use with them.

Route 493 was an oddity, in that it operated entirely within Greater London as a local London Country service in the Orpington area. On 3 September 1978, Swanley RMC1465 is seen at the junction of Chelsfield Lane and Avalon Road. Buses were interworked with trunk route 477, which was the last major LCBS route to operate RMCs early in 1980.

Looking very smart, RF536 has recently been recertified and repainted to keep services going from Kingston Garage on routes 218 and 219. It is seen on a rush hour working of the latter to Weybridge BAC Works at Ashley Road, Walton-On-Thames, on 6 September 1978. Alas, a final solution to the problem of replacing the aged RFs on these routes was found by reallocating them to Norbiton Garage, where Leyland Nationals replaced them at the end of March 1979.

Later the same evening, an almost empty RMC1496 from Leatherhead Garage crosses Epsom Downs on route 406, shortly before their final demise on this trunk route. More than ten years later, this RMC was one of a number refurbished to work Docklands Express route X15 from Upton Park Garage.

A very battered RMC1512, complete with hand-written G4 'blind', stands in for an OPO vehicle when working from Hatfield Garage on this local route in Bridge Road, Welwyn Garden City, on 13 September 1978. Note also the ill-fitting NBC bus stop flag affixed to the LT post on the right. As mentioned earlier, this RMC would be the last one in LCBS service almost eighteen months later.

At Hatfield Garage itself the same day, a forlorn-looking RMC1482 has been out of action for almost a year, and although sold back to LT in 1979, was never used again by them and scrapped in October 1981.

A handful of RMLs remained at Harlow Garage, used to stand in for defective OPO types. Also on 13 August 1978, RML2352 is seen on Town Service 808, in the new development of Katherines, where houses may be seen still under construction in the background.

The last deliveries of DMSs, which were of the supposedly improved Leyland B20 type, had now been made, and on 14 September 1978, one of them, DMS2378 which had replaced RTs on route 89 in April, accompanies Bromley RM1722 in the new Lewisham Bus Station. The latter is working one of the many 'shorts' on route 47 which ran between there and its southernmost destination, Farnborough.

Barking was by now the last garage to operate RTs in service, and here on 15 September 1978, a group of them are seen in the garage yard. RT3871, nearest the camera on the right, is a trainer but will eventually be preserved and is today part of the London Bus Company's splendid heritage fleet. RT2293, blinded for their final route, the 62, is also nicely preserved today.

On the same day, RCL2251, still in Lincoln green livery, is seen in Grays Bus Station and is one of a handful still based in Grays helping out for defunct OPO vehicles. Two Eastern National Leyland Nationals are seen behind it. London Country was by now acquiring hundreds of these, which looked exactly the same as the Eastern National ones in NBC green livery, thereby submerging the fleet into standardised NBC monotony.

Changes to various London bus routes at the end of October 1978 saw the withdrawal of the long-established Sunday-only route 59. On 16 September 1978, Streatham RM671 arrives at its southern extremity, Old Coulsdon, Tudor Rose. The route No.59 reappeared serving the Brighton Road in the 1980s; today it runs from King's Cross to Streatham Hill daily.

A visit to Aldenham Works on 21 September 1978 sees newly overhauled RM1070, just done for the third time, accompanying an ailing DMS173. The latter should have been due, at seven years old, for its first overhaul, but was rejected as defective and sold for scrap in April 1979. SMS734, visible on the right, has just been overhauled but will fare little better – it was withdrawn just two years later.

On **7** October 1978, Sutton RM1402 escorts a DMS through Angel Hill cutting, Sutton. Route 164 was converted to these awful vehicles at the end of March 1979 (and the 164A withdrawn) and this area would be cursed with them well into the 1980s.

With another crew-operated DM on route 134 for company at the McDonald Road stand at Archway Station, Holloway DM1053 lays over on route 17 on 10 October 1978. This trolleybus replacement route was withdrawn at the end of the month and replaced by an extension of the already circuitous route 45 from King's Cross. However, the situation would be reversed in August 1985, when the 45 was cut back and the 17 reintroduced, but continuing from Holborn to London Bridge, rather than Camberwell Green as before. It still exists in that form today.

By October 1978, the unreliability of the DMSs had become beyond a joke, with plans afoot to actually revert some of the routes they worked to crew RM operation. The first DMS route to do so was the Sunday 279A, on which Tottenham DMS431 is seen at Edmonton, Regal, on 8 October 1978, three weeks before the change.

Route 87 was
the penultimate
RT-operated route.
Barking RT2671
heads west along
Rush Green Road,
Romford, on
21 October 1978,
a week before RMs
took over. This long-
established route,
which at this period
ran from Harold
Hill to Rainham
via Romford and
Barking, no longer
exists today.

A surprise in 1977 was the purchase by London Country of ten Plaxton-bodied AEC Reliances, new in 1972, from Barton Transport of Nottingham. Despite having coach-style body shells, they were fitted out as buses with three-and-two seating, originally for 64 passengers. London Country downseated them to 60, and although they were primarily meant for use on school or industrial contracts, they found their way on to normal stage-carriage bus routes and also Green Line coach services. Thus RN1 is seen at Hyde Park Corner working route 714 from Dorking Garage on 26 October 1978.

Another visit to Aldenham Works on 2 November 1978 finds newly-delivered Metrobus M9, fourth of the production batch, accompanying RT2399, in temporary use as a staff bus. The Metrobus would enter service replacing DMSs at Fulwell Garage in March 1979, and see some twenty years' service in London.

Also at Aldenham that day, DMS1248 had been completely burnt out when working route 280A from Sutton Garage in August 1978. Ironically, it was the first of the batch of these dreadful vehicles to have been bodied by Metro-Cammell, and was new in 1972.

Meanwhile, the surviving MBs, all now in use only on Central London Red Arrow services, were being given overhauls. Owing to the fear of bodywork distortion, their bodies were not removed from their chassis during the process, as may be seen here. This is MBA458 which was taken in for overhaul in September, and outshopped to Walworth Garage in December. They lasted until the summer of 1981, when they were replaced by new Leyland Nationals.

One of Aldenham's fitters puts some finishing touches to newly-overhauled RM30 before it goes into the oven to be varnished. This stocknumber had been on 'Works Float' since mass overhauls of RMs began in the summer of 1963. A reduction in their intake at this period led to it, and some of its fellows, being released into service.

Showing the ex-Bournemouth Sightseeing Fleetlines in 'winter mode' with their tops re-fitted, DMO7 passes Monument Station on 6 November 1978.

Seen approaching Highgate Station, Ford Thames Trader towing lorry 1987F tows a defunct DMS597 from Holloway Garage to Aldenham Works for repairs on 8 November 1978. The DMS would survive another two years in service.

Christmas Day, 25 December 1978, sees Wandsworth DM2545, which was usually used on route 168, working route 28 instead of its allocated RMs in Kensington Church Street. This was because there had been a spate of attacks on bus crews in the 'bad lands' of Notting Hill and North Kensington at this period, and crews asked for doored buses to give them some measure of protection.

London suffered heavy snowfall over the New Year of 1978/79, which was a godsend to photographers such as me wanting to catch pictures of the last RTs in the snow. On their final route, the 62, Barking RT1301 arrives at Barkingside, Fullwell Cross, on 6 January 1979.

At the end of October 1978, new route 283 was introduced replacing the 279 between Hammond Street and Waltham Cross, and overlapping it as far as Lower Edmonton Station. It was allocated crew-operated DMs, but these were such a disaster that on 2 February 1979, the entire route had to be RM-operated. RM1805 and RM1153 are seen at the latter terminus. The 283 was not a success either, being withdrawn in September 1980 and replaced by a re-extended 279.

Daylight fades on Sunday, 11 February 1979 as Barking RT624 sets off from its garage to work a District Line rail replacement service between Plaistow and Bromley-By-Bow Stations. This was the last time during the RTs' forty years of normal service that an RT was used in this capacity, and this same RT would be the last one in service just under two months later. Most ironically, however, RT624 is today part of the Ensignbus Heritage Fleet, and was used on a number of occasions during 2014 and 2015 as an 'extra' on routes such as the 15 when the Underground was closed due to strike action.

More heavy snow struck London in mid-February. This caused havoc all the more, since local authority workers were on strike, meaning that roads were not gritted. Chaos reigned particularly on hills, notably on the Northern Heights. Here, on 14 February 1979, Wood Green DMS889 and DMS899 have had to be abandoned whilst working route W2 on Crouch Hill. Interestingly, Routemasters working route 41 on nearby Crouch End Hill, however, had no problems negotiating that equally steep hill in the snow.

On 24 February 1979, Kingston RF471 passes beneath the low bridge carrying the London & South Western main line at Littleworth Common near Esher which obliged routes 218 and 219 to be single-deck operated. Five weeks later, Leyland Nationals took over the two routes.

On the same day, RF495, also from Kingston Garage, stands in for a BL on route 216 when seen at Sunbury Church. Note the unusual treatment of its 'bullseye' filler cap.

1979 marked the 150th anniversary of George Shillibeer starting up the first bus services in London. To mark it, twelve RMs were overhauled in an approximation of Shillibeer's dark green and yellow livery, and the last DM (DM2646) also received it. This vehicle and eight of the RMs are seen at their official launch at the City's Guildhall on 2 March 1979. The other four RMs are out of the picture on the right.

A surprise at this period was the painting of training RCL2232 in red livery, whereas others of the class so employed retained London Country or NBC green. On 16 March 1979, this view at Fulwell Cross nicely shows its rear emergency exit as well as its platform doors. It remained unique in being used as a trainer in red, but in the latter part of 1980, forty of the RCLs (all by now returned to London Transport), including this one, were overhauled in red livery and used to replace DMs on route 149. In the process, however, they lost their platform doors.

At this period, sixteen RMs were overhauled in a special red and yellow livery for the 'Shoplinker' service, which served the West End and Kensington High Street stores at a flat fare of 30p. On 18 March 1979, RM2188 and RM2146 are posed for a press launch opposite Selfridges in Oxford Street. The 'shop blinds' attached to their windows were there for this occasion only. The service was not a success, and withdrawn at the end of September.

Even before the last RTs had been withdrawn, the first DMSs were reaching the Yorkshire scrapyards. Also on 18 March 1979, the gutted skeleton of DMS296, stripped of any usable parts that can help keep others in service, is dumped in West Ham Garage. A few days later it was towed away to Wombwell Diesels; good riddance to bad rubbish!

The British Airways express service from the West London Air Terminal to Heathrow Airport was rendered obsolete by the extension of the Piccadilly Line to Heathrow late in 1977, and finally withdrawn at the end of March 1979. On 24 March 1979, a week before the end, a group of Routemaster coaches stand at WLAT. All passed to London Transport where most saw use as staff buses or driver trainers.

On a wet 29 March 1979, Tottenham DMS1283 stands at the Finsbury Park Station terminus of route 106, which had received these contraptions in August 1972. So disastrous were they that, two days after this picture was taken, the route was re-converted to crew RM operation. This DMS, however, saw several years' further service with Derby Corporation after sale by LT later in 1979.

By 30 March 1979, apart from those at Northfleet on route 480, only a handful of London Country RMLs remained in service. One was Windsor RML2411, seen in the company of one of the new generation of Green Line AEC Reliance coaches and an SM in Windsor Bus Station.

In the adjacent London Country Windsor Garage, MB4, the last remaining Strachans-bodied member of its class, which had been exchanged with London Transport for XMB15, is amongst a group of withdrawn vehicles, including a standard MB, an RF and even an RP.

30 March 1979 was the last day in service of London Transport's RFs. At Staines, Moor Lane terminus, Kingston RF512 is on the scheduled allocation on route 218, whilst RF522 stands in for a BL on route 216. BL34 on this route and a Leyland National on route 116 complete the picture.

Some of the last DM-types built, B20 crew-operated DMs, replaced earlier examples at Cricklewood Garage on route 16 and 16A during 1978. The last one, DM2646 adorned in Shillibeer livery, joined them. On 1 April 1979, it sets off from its home garage bearing adverts for more successful Leyland types – the National and the B15 Titan, both of which were now being delivered to London Transport in considerable numbers. The 16 and 16A converted to RML operation in May 1980, largely using ex-London Country examples.

Also in Shillibeer livery, Norbiton RM2130 heads a group of other RMs on routes 65 and 71 whose services have been disrupted by the infamous Petersham Hole, a road subsidence in Petersham Road between Richmond and Ham, on 2 April 1979. Buses had to be terminated either side of the hole, with their passengers walking between them to change buses and continue their journeys.

On 7 April 1979, the end has finally come for London's RTs. The last one, RT624, is seen in Barkingside High Street about to make its final run back to Barking. Walthamstow DMS2032 on route 275 follows.

After the last RTs had run in to Barking Garage (after being substituted by RMs) around lunchtime that day, a farewell cavalcade over route 62 from Barking to Barkingside and back was run featuring six of Barking's last RTs. Heading it, however, was the newly-restored 'RT1', which although carrying the original body built in 1939 for the first RT, is actually mounted on the chassis of post-war RT1420. This combination had served as a mobile instruction unit for bus maintenance staff since 1955 (as service vehicle 1037J) and had languished in store at West Ham Garage until as late as 1978. Though, of course, a splendid job was done privately in restoring the body, it is perhaps unfortunate that the vehicle was not preserved officially by London Transport. It might then have been married up with a 'pre-war' 2RT2 chassis, of which a couple were still available, which would have been more 'original' than the combination seen here.

Seen arriving at Battersea Park on Easter Sunday, 15 April 1979, Battersea DMS2227 works route 137A, the special route which ran on summer Sundays and bank holidays between Sloane Square and Battersea Pleasure Gardens.

An unusual vehicle hired to London Transport for special route 74Z between Baker Street Station and London Zoo is ex-Devon General open-top AEC Regent V No.507. It is seen in Gloucester Place also on 15 April 1979.

After three and a half years of crew DM operation on route 24, these awful vehicles were swapped with Stonebridge Park Garage's RMLs on route 18. A scruffy Chalk Farm DM1150 is seen at Warren Street Station on their last day on the 24, 21 April 1979.

Somewhat oddly, ex-London Country RML2442 has been overhauled in red livery, only to be allocated initially to driver training duties. It is seen in the company of Red Arrow MBAs in Walworth Garage on 22 April 1979. It finally would re-enter passenger service replacing DMs at Cricklewood on routes 16 and 16A in May 1980.

For some reason, the route number 296 was used twice during the 1970s for 'experimental' routes which did not last long. On 5 May 1979, Finchley DMS2012 has just set off from North Finchley's Tally Ho! Bus Station on this version of the 296, which ran from Copthall Stadium, Mill Hill, to North Finchley and was allocated just one bus, which here is turning short at Hendon Central. The route lasted only from 31 March to 28 September 1979, and had been introduced at the request of Barnet Council.

Arsenal have won the FA Cup again, and on Sunday, 13 May 1979, a shabby Holloway DM1053 working route 104, is diverted off its normal route along Upper Street while the team are being feted at Islington Town Hall. It is seen turning from Canonbury Road into Essex Road. Note the T-shape advert on its offside, necessitating the repositioning of its bullseye. Such advertisements for cigarettes on buses are of course taboo today! Meanwhile, route 104 reverted to Routemaster operation in the spring of 1981, only to convert to DMS OPO eighteen months later and then be withdrawn three years after that.

The large Country Area garage at Garston had always had spare space to store new or withdrawn buses, and continued to do so in London Country days. On 19 May 1979, a very sorry-looking RML2432, which had been out of action for over a year, accompanies AN60 and AN107, both of which are awaiting overhaul. The RML would be sold to London Transport in July and re-entered service in 1980 after overhaul, lasting into the mid-2000s. The two ANs remained in LCBS service well into the 1980s.

At Chelsham Garage on 20 May 1979, RMC1487 and RMC1501 flank an engineless RCL2243, and are three of several withdrawn Routemasters stored there following the withdrawal of the type from route 403. Though all three seen here passed to London Transport, only the RCL would see service with them. RMC1487 was actually painted red for training duties, but then sold privately without seeing such use.

Apart from a nasty dent on its nearside front, East Grinstead XF3 looks smart in NBC corporate livery when seen on route 424 in Smallfield Road, Horley, on 24 May 1979. Some of this class had now been withdrawn, though others survived until 1981 – the last ex-London Transport buses in the London Country fleet.

On the same day, ex-South Wales AEC Swift SMW3 is seen working route 426 from Crawley Garage at Horley Station. The days of these vehicles were numbered now, too.

Just one RF now remained in London Country service, and therefore outlived the London Transport ones. This was modernised ex-Green Line RF202 based at Northfleet Garage, seen here working route 490 at New Ash Green, also on 24 May 1979. A BN-class Bristol LH passes in the other direction. Later, the RF was used as a heritage vehicle, and eventually passed into preservation.

London Country attempted to revive the flagging fortunes of its Green Line coach services by providing them with new, luxury coaches. On 29 May 1979, one of these, Hertford-based Plaxton Supreme-bodied AEC Reliance RS115, is seen on route 715 at Wood Green Shopping City. These coaches were only leased by London Country, for a period of five years. Green Line's fortunes did not really improve thanks to them – increasing traffic congestion saw to that!

By 2 June 1979, few SMSs remained in service with London Transport. One of their last regular allocations was on route S2 from Dalston Garage, on which SMS708 departs from Clapton Pond. The blind display 'Bromley Stn' is misleading – it really refers to Bromley-By-Bow Station. Leyland Nationals replaced the SMSs on this route in November 1979, but this one survived to prop up Red Arrow services in 1980/81, being one of the very last of this unfortunate class in service.

An array of defunct London Country vehicles dumped at Grays Garage on 4 July 1979; nearest the camera are RF239, an engineless RML2416 and a very dead Leyland National, with one of the ex-Ribble Burlingham-bodied Leyland Titan PD3s of the LR class that London Country had acquired for training duties on the extreme right. The RML was sold to London Transport a few days after this picture was taken, and overhauled as a red bus some months later. The very heavily cannibalised RML on the left is RML2345, which had been off the road since March 1975, but it too was rescued by LT and returned to service after overhaul in May 1981 – both of these RMLs survived in service until 2005.

Not so lucky is RML2423, which though mechanically and bodily complete was sold by London Country, along with RML2424, to Wombwell Diesels and scrapped. Its skeleton is seen there on 5 July 1979. Rumour has it that LCBS sold the two for scrap to prompt LT to buy their remaining Routemasters, since the latter had apparently been haggling over their purchase price. Whether this is true or not, the ruse worked.

Equally sad is this line of RFs, also at Wombwell. Since they were equipped for one person operation, there had been hopes of selling them for further use – but to prospective buyers, by now they were simply too old!

Few people shed any tears for the SM and DM types now following the RTs and RFs to the scrapyard. SMS801 and DMS1612 are seen here; the latter had been withdrawn owing to fire damage at the rear.

Most of Wombwell's victims at this period were still RTs, especially since the last had been withdrawn from service three months previously. After their bodies had been stripped of reusable metal, they were removed from their chassis and ended up like this.

In complete contrast to the previous scenes, brand new London Country Atlantean AN200 is seen in Wakley Street, Islington, on a road run of exhibits marking the Shillibeer 150th anniversary from London Wall to a rally in Hyde Park on 8 July 1979.

SMSs displaced by new Leyland Nationals were in some cases used to help out ailing MBAs on Red Arrow services – SMS756 has been sent to Gillingham Street when seen on route 507 at Victoria Bus Station, also on 8 July 1979. A Bow DMS on the original route 10, which conversion to that type destroyed, arrives in the background.

In the Clapham Garage store on 9 July 1979, brand new Leyland Nationals LS327 and LS315 contrast with withdrawn SMS710.

On 14 July 1979, SMS603 is one that had been recertified upon reaching seven years in service rather than overhauled, and is seen at Plaistow Broadway working from West Ham Garage on the now normally DMS-operated route 241. Withdrawn in early 1980, it was exported to Malta where it spent many more years in service.

Also at Plaistow Broadway that day, West Ham DMS653 is unusually working as a crew DM on route 262, which would revert to RM operation in October.

Seen in Aldenham Works on 2 August 1979, RML2595 is having a new roof fitted after losing its original through being driven under the notorious low bridge carrying the Great Northern main line over Stroud Green Road at Finsbury Park Station. As may be seen, the roof was peeled back like the lid of a sardine can, with no damage at all to the RML's windows. The 'new' roof was in fact a green one, thus proving that at least some of the parts from the Country RMLs scrapped at Wombwell must have been returned to London Transport for such use.

Unbelievably, the same driver – a fitter at Holloway Garage – who had deroofed RML2595 at Finsbury Park did the same to DM1757 on 14 August 1979 just a few weeks later! I saw it happen, and as I luckily always had a camera with me, I could record the event. Unlike the RML, which emerged from the other side of the bridge minus its roof, the DM was well and truly stuck under the bridge, and as may be seen, its flimsy windows have been smashed and the bodywork distorted too. It happened in the evening rush hour, and the Leyland National following on the 236's rush hour extension to Stroud Green is marooned behind it. Despite the DM being blinded for route 4, it was not in service as it had broken down and was being driven back 'dead' to the garage. The force of the collision with the bridge wrecked its suspension too, thus it was withdrawn – the first crew-operated DM to perish.

Green Line routes were now being re-cast too, and new route 732 replaced parts of the old 716. On 25 August 1979, Hatfield Leyland National bus LNB44 has been put on this route and is seen in Ballards Lane, North Finchley.

By this period, some of the earlier DMSs had received Aldenham overhauls. One was DMS100, seen working from Holloway Garage on route 239 in Dartmouth Park Hill on 16 August 1979. This did not save it from withdrawal and sale for scrap two years later, however.

On 26 August 1979, the Petersham Hole is still disrupting bus services. By now, new route 265 has replaced the Leatherhead to Chessington section of the 71, and here Kingston BL53 stands in Sandpits Road at the southern side of the obstruction.

Another route which had changed in the south-western corner of London Transport's area, as we saw earlier, was the 237. It was cut back from Chertsey to Sunbury in January 1978. At that end, new London Country route 459 replaced it. Also on 26 August 1979, Addlestone SM131 is seen working it in Feltham Hill Road. This SM was withdrawn in November 1979, but exported to the USA a few months later.

Representing one of the three new types of London Transport double-decker which would oust most DMSs during the coming decade, Fulwell Metrobus M52 leaves Hounslow Bus Station for Tolworth on route 281 on the same day. Unfortunately, this attractive livery with white window surrounds on the upper deck was not perpetuated on most of the class, which were originally just plain red.

Usually used on trunk route 29 from Enfield to Victoria, Palmers Green 'Shillibeer' RM2186 has been fielded on route 102 on August Bank Holiday Monday, 27 August 1979. It is seen here leaving Chingford Station for Golders Green – the driver has forgotten to change his blind.

On 29 August 1979, Gillingham Street MBA549 is one of the few survivors of this class when seen at Millbank about to cross Lambeth Bridge on Red Arrow route 507. Most of them by now had been given Aldenham overhauls, but for some reason this one was not done until 1980, and lasted just a year in service afterwards.

Windsor-operated route 407 was a last outpost of London Country RML operation in the Slough Area. On 30 August 1979, RML2348 terminates at Cippenham, which was one of the westernmost points served by the operator. RMLs lingered here into the first weeks of 1980.

In its final weeks, the Shoplinker service lost the '30p' blind display (which alluded to its flat fare) since this apparently caused confusion with normal route 30, which the service paralleled between Marble Arch and South Kensington. On 12 September 1979, Stockwell RM2207 is seen in Harrington Road at the latter location.

Bearing the new NBC Green Line livery, Dorking RP42 approaches Hyde Park Corner working an apparently empty 714. 'Shillibeer' RM2208 follows in the background. By now, a number of RPs had already been withdrawn, although this one survived until late 1983.

At Aldenham Works on 16 September 1979, B20 DMS2433 is yet another to have suffered a serious engine fire – ironically when working from Ponders End Garage on route 107 which passed the works. Somewhat surprisingly, it was repaired and overhauled there, only to be withdrawn after just a few weeks back in service in 1982, which says it all for these horrible buses.

Also at Aldenham that day, SMS328 has been wrecked in a collision when working from Uxbridge Garage in June. One of the relatively few of this equally awful class to be overhauled at Aldenham, not surprisingly it was not repaired and went for scrap a few weeks after this picture was taken.

In addition to Uxbridge, Edgware Garage retained SMSs longer than most others. Their SMS742 is seen on the 240 in Brent Street, Hendon, on 22 September 1979. After withdrawal late in 1980, this SMS was one of a number donated to help in relief operations for a serious earthquake in Italy. The vehicles were driven all the way there by volunteer LT drivers. Edgware would be the last LT garage to operate SM-types in the suburbs, the last of which perished early in 1981.

By now, the fifty forward-entrance Routemasters delivered to Northern General in 1964/65, along with the prototype ex-RMF1254 which they had bought from London Transport, were being withdrawn. EUP407B is one of two acquired by Obsolete Fleet, and hired to LT for their Round London Sightseeing Tour. It has been given the fleet number RMF2762. So desperate were LT to acquire Routemasters at this period, that a batch was bought from Northern General in December 1979, with others following in 1980. It had been intended to operate them on routes 26 and 45. Sadly, however, they were rejected for a variety of reasons. This very lucky shot down the 'Dilly on 28 September 1979 sees 'RMF2762' in the company of LT's unique FRM1.

Very early DMSs were now being withdrawn upon their replacement in the west by Metrobuses and in the east by Leyland B15 Titans. On 29 September 1979, however, Leyton DMS3 is still at work on route 55 when seen in Hoe Street, Walthamstow. It had had an Aldenham overhaul early in 1978, and when route 55 reverted to crew RM operation at the end of January 1981, was transferred to Upton Park. It lasted only until October that year when it was withdrawn. After a year in store, it was sold for scrap.

One of the last pockets of SM operation for London Country was the Dartford area. Locally-based SM514 is still in Lincoln green livery when seen at Dartford Market Place on 1 October 1979, working route 486, much of which ran within the Greater London area. Some of these vehicles struggled on until early 1981; all had been withdrawn by the end of the year.

Failures of relatively new B20 DMSs at Bexleyheath Garage meant that members of the first batch of single-door, 45-seat SMs which had been in store at Clapham had to be sent there for route 132. SM5 and SM45 are seen at Bexleyheath Clocktower also on 1 October 1979. Note the makeshift blinds on both. DMSs returned to the route in November.

At Southall Garage on 2 October 1979, brand new Metrobus M88 contrasts with DMS721, both working route 282. Here, as elsewhere, Metrobuses and Titans replaced DMSs on a gradual, garage-by-garage basis.

Minus engine, gearbox, blindbox, front dome, a number of windows and also seats, London Country RML2345 looks for all the world a goner when seen at Grays Garage on 21 October 1979. It had in fact been earmarked for scrap at the end of 1977, but could not be towed to Yorkshire as it had no front wheels. They appear to be on it here, but not connected by an axle! In the end it was rescued by London Transport and overhauled at Aldenham in the spring of 1981, lasting in service until July 2005. Here, it is accompanied by small ECW-bodied Bristol LH BN41, and two withdrawn MBs.

Continuing with London Country's efforts to revive Green Line's fortunes, Duple Britannia-bodied AEC Reliance RB99, based at Addlestone, works new Green Line route 734 when seen in Park Road, Hornsey, on 1 November 1979. This route followed the existing 715 from Hertford to Wood Green, then continued to Addlestone via Muswell Hill, Brent Cross Shopping Centre and Heathrow Airport. Sadly, it was not a success due largely to being sabotaged by traffic congestion.

Seen in Romford town centre on 10 November 1979, London Transport's ECW-bodied Bristol LH BL7 is seen on the now very long 247, running from Epping to Brentwood. It has recently been repainted in this rather drab all-red livery.

Also repainted in an all-red livery, Peckham Metro-Scania MD4 is seen on route 36 at the northern end of Vauxhall Bridge on 8 December 1979. By now, these vehicles had proved themselves to be too costly both in fuel and maintenance, and the 36 group of routes reverted to RM operation early in 1980. Those MDs still serviceable were redeployed to OPO routes in South-East London, but all were withdrawn by the summer of 1983.

Also on the way out now were the AEC Swifts that had been diverted to London Country from South Wales Transport. SMW5 stands outside its home garage, St. Albans, also on 8 December 1979.

Seen at Dartford Garage on 9 December 1979. London Country P10 is a 1971 Plaxton-bodied AEC Reliance coach that had been acquired from National Travel South East in 1977 for tours and private hire work.

More typical of the London Country fleet as the 1970s drew to a close was Leyland National SNB333, seen the same day at Joyce Green Hospital working from Northfleet Garage on route 480, where they have finally replaced the RMLs.

Brand new Plaxton Supreme-bodied AEC Reliance RS140 loads up in East Street, Barking, working from Grays Garage on route 723 on 31 December 1979. It is a far cry from the RT and Routemaster Green Line coaches that worked this route in the 1950s and 1960s.

At Barking Garage that same New Year's Eve, brand new Leyland B15 Titan T113 contrasts with DMS303 and RM1555. These somewhat ironically replaced RMs and DMSs alike here early in 1980, starting with the RTs' final route, the 62, which had only received RMs in April.

Quite remarkably, as dusk was falling on the last day of the 1970s, Plumstead RT4566 appeared on training duties as I was walking from Plumstead Station to the Woolwich Transport Museum on the nearby industrial estate. Its driver stopped for me here in Nathan Way, telling me that this was the RT's very last run as its licence expired that night. This was also the very last London Transport RT used on driver training duties, and also the very last bus I photographed in the 1970s – how appropriate!